BASEBALL INSIDE OUT

BASEBALL

· Inside Out ·

WINNING THE GAMES

WITHIN THE GAMES

Bruce Shlain

VIKING

VIKING
Published by the Penguin Group
Viking Penguin, a division of Penguin Books USA Inc.,
375 Hudson Street, New York, New York 10014, U.S.A.
Penguin Books Ltd, 27 Wrights Lane, London W8 5TZ, England
Penguin Books Australia Ltd, Ringwood, Victoria, Australia
Penguin Books Canada Ltd, 10 Alcorn Avenue, Suite 300,
Toronto, Ontario, Canada M4V 3B2
Penguin Books (N.Z.) Ltd, 182–190 Wairau Road,
Auckland 10, New Zealand

Penguin Books Ltd, Registered Offices:
Harmondsworth, Middlesex, England

First published in 1992 by Viking Penguin,
a division of Penguin Books USA Inc.

1 3 5 7 9 10 8 6 4 2

LIBRARY OF CONGRESS CATALOGING IN PUBLICATION DATA
Shlain, Bruce.
Baseball inside out:
winning the games within the games/
by Bruce Shlain.
p   cm.   ISBN 0-670-83506-4
1. Baseball. 2. Baseball—History. I. Title.
GV867.S616 1992   796.357—dc20   91-31388

Printed in the United States of America
Set in Times Roman
Designed by Jessica Shatan

Acknowledgments

I wish to thank all those in baseball, literally too numerous to mention, who parted the curtains by sharing their experiences with me. Sincere thanks also to my agent at ICM, Bob Tabian. I want to express my gratitude as well for the efforts of several people at Viking–assistant editors Lekha Menon and Nicole Guisto, for their constant help; Barbara Elovic, for her meticulous copyediting; editor Roger Devine, for his vision and encouragement in the initial stages of the manuscript; and my editor Al Silverman, whose tireless and invaluable contribution made this book into a real collaboration.

Contents

Introduction: Games Within Games

Perhaps baseball's ultimate appeal is that it can be appreciated on so many different levels, from the heroic to the comic, from the obvious to the subtle. Within each baseball contest, there are games within the game, and some of them are not confined to the playing field. As my old English professor at the University of Michigan, Donald Hall, wrote, "Baseball is best played in the theater of the mind"— and it is the rare ballgame that does not have some mythlike reverberation in the memory of some fan.

Neither does it take the epic, pressurized struggles of a pennant race, playoff, or World Series to provide such moments of baseball revelation. Even a game in the Senior League in Florida, between ex-major leaguers, can flash dimensions.

One day in Winter Haven's Chain o' Lakes Park in 1989, Jim Willoughby was pitching for the Super Sox, a team managed in the early part of the season by Bill Lee, who was once known as Spaceman. In the eighth inning, Lee lifted Willoughby in favor of Pedro Borbon, a former member of the 1975 Reds, and Borbon blew the game. The sequence of events was a near remake of the classic seventh game of the '75 Series. In that game, Willoughby had been taken out for a pinch-hitter in the bottom of the eighth with the score tied. Rookie left-hander Jim Burton came in to try and hold the Reds in the top of the ninth. He walked the first man and the winning run scored on a two-out pop-fly single by Joe Morgan.

For years afterward, off-season lulls in bar talk throughout New

England were broken by the proclamation, "They shoulda left Willoughby in!" The game that day in the Senior League was a perfect dose of *déjà vu* for the fan with an ear for hearing the notes and phrases from some other game within the game.

The same happens every time the arch-rival Red Sox and Yankees play each other with something at stake. When Bucky Dent homered to beat the Red Sox in the 1978 one-game playoff, there was that curse of the Bambino again, harking back to Harry Frazee's sale of Red Sox pitcher Babe Ruth in 1919 to the Yankees. Likewise, when the Dodgers and Giants get into a barnburner out West, time and coast-to-coast distances evaporate as fans remember emotionally charged confrontations in Ebbets Field or the Polo Grounds. In sports, decades can seem like minutes.

Players whose uniform numbers may have been long retired live again when certain plays arise. A third baseman makes a diving stab and pops, catlike, to his feet to throw out a runner, and those who saw Brooks Robinson will be reminded of how often he turned such dazzling plays into mere routine. When Ken Griffey, Jr., leaps up against the fence with otherworldly grace to catch a sure homer, many still recall the reappearing image of the young Willie Mays. The fans are in many respects the game's true keepers of the flame, because it is in their interior stadiums that baseball endlessly recycles itself.

In the same manner, when record feats and streaks of the game are challenged or broken, the record-holders are automatically resurrected. When Don Mattingly hit home runs in eight consecutive games in 1987 he tied the record of the forgotten Dale Long, who enjoyed that brief but nonetheless unexpected and appreciated moment in the sun back in 1957. And when Pete Rose went on his record forty-four-game National League hitting streak in 1978, he passed the Boston Braves' Tommy Holmes, who once had a thirty-seven-game streak, thus giving his name national exposure for the first time since 1945, the year of his streak.

In the middle of a woeful season for the Yankees in 1990, pitcher Andy Hawkins threw a no-hitter and managed to lose 4–0. His misfortune reacquainted fans with the only other man to lose a nine-inning no-hitter, Ken Johnson of the Astros—he lost his no-no 1–0 in 1964. Johnson was plagued by puny run support throughout his career. They even staged a "Runs for Johnson Night"; any woman with a run in her stocking got into the ballpark free. That night Jim Bunning beat Johnson with a one-hitter.

Whatever ballplayers accomplish over a season or a career is represented by numbers set in stone—these remain more meaningful in baseball than in any other sport. One reason is that other games have changed so much that it has made a mockery of old-time record-keeping. In hockey, Wayne Gretzky broke Gordie Howe's mark for career points (goals and assists) in less than half the time it took Howe. But hockey is a different sport in Gretzky's time than it was in Howe's. Baseball, despite artificial turf, domed stadiums, night games, and split-finger fastballs, is essentially unchanged from when Ruth and Cobb played it. A groundball hit in the hole, if fielded cleanly by the shortstop and thrown hard and accurately to first, still nips the fastest runner by half a step. The standards of excellence remain consistent; no other game can match baseball's equivalent plateaus—sixty-one home runs, a .400 average, or a fifty-six-game hitting streak.

Every ballplayer is playing a game within the game, competing against not only all the players he faces, but all the players in his league. And the great ones compete with the upper echelon of ballplayers throughout history. Ted Williams went into the last day of the 1941 season hitting .39995, which would have been rounded off to .400. He could have sat it out. But he approached that last day, a doubleheader against the Senators, as an ultimate challenge, a private test. It would tell him how he measured up against all the great hitters throughout time. Williams went six for eight, one of his line drives busting a loudspeaker high off the right-field wall. He finished at .406.

Even though baseball is a team sport, each player basically takes care of his job in an isolated fashion; the "team" does not face a 3-2 pitch in the clutch—a single individual does. When Detroit's Al Kaline was nearing the end of his celebrated career, he sometimes sat in the dugout and looked out on the field, "thinking about me, me, me, my batting average, my fielding average," he told Ira Berkow of *The New York Times*. "Oh, sure, you care about the team. You have to. But in the end you're worried about you."

Kaline retired with 399 home runs. Since he had over 3,000 hits, he could have been the first American League player to combine 400 homers and 3,000 hits. But he decided that when he got his three-thousandth hit, that would be it. So Carl Yastrzemski became the first to do it.

I would have liked Kaline to have had that double 400–3000 because as I was growing up in Detroit he was my first baseball hero. There is a pronounced tendency among many young baseball fans to attach themselves to one ballplayer, and that person becomes a kind of totem or alter ego. You pin your boyhood hopes on him. You thrill to his successes and hurt when he fails. For actor Bill Murray, growing up in Chicago, it was Ernie Banks. He named his son Homer Banks Murray after the announcer's call of a four-bagger by his hero—"Homer, Banks." It is for the same reason that Bob Costas still carries a baseball card of Mickey Mantle in his wallet.

Most star ballplayers understand this hero worship. Joe DiMaggio was once asked how he was able to always play so hard. He said that each time he played there was somebody seeing him for the last time, and some young boy seeing him for the first time. Why was it Kaline for me? He was the same kind of quiet player as DiMaggio. He didn't, of course, have DiMaggio's obvious physical gifts. In fact, his feet always hurt like hell from a bone deformity, but he made the game look easy by working so hard. It never bothered me that he lacked charisma, because there was no player you could watch and learn more about how to win baseball games. Some players channel all their pride and will to win into the game, with nothing left over for display. I can still see the young Kaline, having just hit a double, standing on second base in the sun, arms akimbo, hips to one side, head tilted to the other, unmoving, with the cheers ringing in his ears.

In 1962, a certain incident in New York began for me what I suppose might be called "the Kaline thing." The season had opened at Tiger Stadium with Frank "Taters" Lary, the noted "Yankee-killer," pitching against the Yankees on a cold, blustery day. I was ten years old, listening to Ernie Harwell on a transistor radio. Lary won the game, and even had the key hit, a triple, but late in the game he threw a curveball with his arm in the wrong position and was lost for the year. He was, in fact, never the same pitcher. I was beginning to understand how you could win the game, but still lose in a big way.

Lary's injury meant that lanky left-hander Hank Aguirre, normally a reliever and one of the worst hitting pitchers in baseball history (he went two for eighty over one memorable stretch) would step into the rotation. His first big start was against New York in Yankee Stadium that May. He pitched brilliantly. The Tigers were leading New York 2–1 in the bottom of the ninth with two Yankees on and two out. Up came Elston Howard and he popped a fly to short right field, too deep for the second baseman. Respecting Howard's power to the opposite field, Kaline was playing deep in right. The runners were moving. The ball was sinking as Kaline came faster and faster. If it dropped in, the Yankees would win. At the last split second Kaline lunged and caught the ball in the webbing, his momentum carrying him through three rapid somersaults, like a revved-up washing machine. Somehow he held onto the ball and the Tigers had won. But Kaline lay there as if shot.

He had broken his collarbone, passing out twice from the pain as he was carried to the locker room. He would miss two months of the season. At the time of the injury, Kaline was leading the league in the Triple Crown categories (even though he played only one hundred games that year, he still hit twenty-nine homers, more than in any other season of his twenty-two-year career). The taste of victory was like a mouthful of ashes. In losing Kaline, the Tigers had lost the war, the game within the game, the pennant race that ticks inside each regular-season contest. But he won my admiration forever.

When you care deeply, you want your hero to lead your team to victories and pennants, but you also always want to see your ballplayer shine and be acknowledged for all the great moments he's given you as a fan.

The kind of game within the game that used to involve the fan with his or her baseball hero when I was a kid may, in some respects, be gone forever. Today the atmosphere around the game has undoubtedly changed. Just who qualifies as a sports hero to today's youth? In a children's poll in 1989, kids picked their male athlete of the year. It wasn't a baseball player; nor was it Michael Jordan or

Magic Johnson or Joe Montana or Wayne Gretzky. It was Hulk Hogan. It should not be so surprising in an age when commercialism has invaded so many areas of sport. For instance, when a ballplayer sells his autograph for twenty dollars at a card show, the young fan may be getting the signature for purely monetary reasons himself, to be able to sell it to someone else at a much higher price years down the road.

Still, baseball fans exist, endure, remember. I remember in the Tigers' '68 championship year when Denny McLain pulled off a triple play against the Baltimore Orioles. There were runners on first and second and nobody out, Boog Powell at the plate. When catcher Bill Freehan came out to the mound, McLain told him, "Don't worry, I'll think of something." Powell lined a shot right at McLain, who reached up, caught it head-high, and spun in the same motion to throw a strike to second. The relay to first completed the triple play.

Over twenty years after the fact, when I asked Bill Freehan about the play, I mentioned that there had been a rain delay during the game, that play had just resumed a few minutes before Powell came up, and that the sun had poked through the clouds just before the pitch. Of course he didn't remember the weather changes; he was busy calling pitches in a pennant race, as he did in over a thousand games. Such inconsequential details are not for a professional athlete's memory bank; they're for the fans who soak it all in.

Why, I have often asked myself, do I remember such things? Consider the twenty-two-inning game between the Yankees and the Tigers in the summer of '62. I began listening to the game with my family at home, then in the car, then at the beach, then back in the car, then again at home, then in the car again, and later still in our favorite Italian restaurant. Shortly after the soup was served, the waiter informed us that the Tigers had loaded the bases with no outs. After they stranded the runners, I was so upset I dropped my spoon. When I leaned down to pick it up, the waiter had taken away my minestrone.

And still the game wore on. I sent the busboy into the kitchen for updates, until the waiter brought a transistor radio (what service!) with dessert. After seven hours, I listened in stunned disbelief as an unknown named Jack Reed won it for New York with a two-run homer. Who the hell was Jack Reed? A youngster named Jim Bouton got the win with seven innings of three-hit relief. That I didn't recall. You could look it up, as Casey Stengel once said. But the rest I remembered.

Could anything be less important now? My father used to indicate as much when we went to games together. He thought the seats were the greatest if they were on the aisle near a concession stand. It's not so much that my dad used to make a casual glutton of himself at a ballgame, but more the way he would leave his seat at the most tense moments in the game. Bases loaded, two outs, and he would go for a hot dog; the lines were shorter than they would be between innings. It was a lesson in proportion and perspective that I couldn't then accept, the view that the outcome of a particular game was relatively insignificant.

Therein lies the beauty of remembering a ballgame from when you were a kid, because so many of the things that pretend to be really important turn out not to be. Baseball never promises relevance; it is only sheer and reliable fact upon fact, strikes and balls, hits and outs, wins and losses—really the only thing that has been so copiously documented for the last hundred years. In the end, I consider myself fortunate that little visual vignettes and sequences from these games have stayed with me.

Some adult fans care for their teams with the same concentrated emotion they felt as children, but I am not one of them. I don't see myself going into the basement ever again to break all the flower pots because the Tigers had just lost a tough game. What did catch my fancy in an enduring way was the game of baseball itself, from the eternal chess game between the pitchers and hitters that hinges on millimeters and milliseconds to the managers feverishly weighing the odds and percentages of various matchups.

Off the field, other games are played, between teammates, with the press, and in the front office where the general managers wheel and deal to assemble winning teams. There is no sport with as many metalevels, inside stratagems, and sheer intangibles. The game's layers can be enjoyably peeled, one after another, like an onion; but while many have attempted to reveal its hidden core, no sport remains so much like life itself, at once so simple and again so hopelessly complex.

PART 1

PITCHERS AND

HITTERS

For All the Marbles

Only baseball can bring a whole season of play down to one pitch, on which the future of the teams and players involved will be forever altered by the outcome. It is the pitcher versus the hitter, and what happens between them. Depending on the swing of the pendulum, it can end up hellfire or everlasting glory. On such at-bats hinge the afterlife of the athlete. Either it's the monument in the city square and the growing car dealership, or naked defeat replayed a dozen different ways, from every angle, at every speed, for the rest of your life. If you think this is hyperbole ask Ralph Branca about the countless out-of-the-way places on this globe where many a well-meaning soul has come up to him during the last forty years, out of the blue, and said, "About that home run you gave up to Bobby Thomson in 1951 . . ."

Sometimes a huge price is paid for playing a boy's game. No player paid a bigger price than Donnie Moore, relief pitcher for the Angels, who took his own life two years after giving up one of the most heartbreaking home runs in baseball history. It was the 1986 playoff and the Angels were up 3–1 against the Red Sox when their ace Mike Witt took a 5–2 lead into the ninth inning. The Red Sox rallied, cutting the Angels' lead to 5–4, with a man on first base and two outs. Donnie Moore was summoned from the bullpen to get the final out against Dave Henderson.

Moore was recovering from a sore shoulder, and was in fact scheduled to receive cortisone shots on that very night, but when the crunch came, he was the best the Angels had. The experienced catcher, Bob Boone, was calling the pitches, and Moore came out smoking. He blew two fastballs past Henderson, who was late on the pitches, and the count was 0–2. The Angels were one strike from the World Series.

The California Angels had never been to the World Series. Neither had their aging owner, Gene Autry, nor had their manager, Gene Mauch, who had managed two of baseball's most notorious collapses—the '64 Phillies and the '82 Angels. They were all one strike away, but in baseball there is no killing the clock, no falling on the ball—you have to throw the sucker over the plate to win.

Moore threw a fastball in the dirt. Then Henderson fouled back the down-breaking split-finger, the pitch that had made Moore the best relief pitcher in baseball in 1985. But this was 1986, and Boone wanted to keep the batter off-balance, and he called for the fastball. Henderson fouled it off, this time almost catching up with it. So Boone called for the split-finger again, and it wasn't the pitcher's best—Moore hung it, and Hendu unbelievably hit it out to give the Red Sox a 6–5 lead.

But the game was not over. The Angels tied the score in their half of the ninth, and then had the bases loaded with only one out, but nothing came of it. In the top of the eleventh, the Red Sox loaded the bases with nobody out, and the last batter Moore faced was—yup—Dave Henderson. He hit a sacrifice fly to bring in the winning run.

The following spring, Moore was asked all the time about his split-finger home-run pitch to Henderson. "More than likely," he said, "I'll think about that until the day I die." He had a lot of time to think about it, as injuries kept him from pitching. When he was out there, he didn't do the job and was frequently, and more and more vehemently, booed by the fans. In September of 1987, when the Angels fell out of the race, their frustrated general manager, Mike Port, was upset that Moore was not working harder on his rehabilitation. Port was quoted as saying: "Instead of whining about hurting his rib cage, he should have been out there earning his money. What do we pay him a million dollars for?"

The first four times he pitched in 1988, Moore blew leads in the opponents' final at-bats. The Angels released him. Moore went down to the minors to try to revive his career, and made it back with the Kansas City Royals in 1989, but they quickly cut him. His baseball career was over. That summer he had to put his $1 million dream house up for sale. He was not broke, but he was not doing well, and his marriage was in serious trouble.

He had been separated from his wife, Tonya, for a month when she returned to the house in Anaheim in July 1989 to show it with Moore to a prospective buyer who never appeared. Moore and his wife argued over Tonya's desire to take their three children away with her. As she was about to leave the house, Moore cracked. He picked up a semiautomatic .45 handgun that his wife had given him for Christmas and shot her in the abdomen, neck, and right shoulder. (She miraculously survived.) Then he put a gun to his own head and pulled the trigger.

"Henderson's homer was what did it," David Pinter, Moore's agent, said. "It sent him over the cliff. He blamed himself for the Angels not going to the World Series. He couldn't get over it."

During the 1989 playoffs, A's short reliever Dennis Eckersley was watching television with a friend when a "20/20" segment came on about Donnie Moore. The friend suggested nervously that perhaps Eckersley shouldn't watch it. He understood his friend's concern, but he said, "I can take it."

Eckersley had, after all, thrown the pitch to Kirk Gibson in 1988 that was hit for one of the most supernaturally improbable home runs in World Series history. It was Game One of the Series, with the A's leading 4–3 in the ninth inning. There was a runner on first, Mike Davis, with two outs, when Gibson hobbled up to the plate on his bad legs as a pinch-hitter.

He barely fouled off the first three pitches, all fastballs; he looked stiff and overmatched. The count went to 3–2, and Eckersley stared in for the sign, still one strike from victory. He went into his windup, kicking his left leg high, then came forward, tilting his body and closing his right eye like a gunslinger before sighting the plate for his whiplash delivery.

The pitch was a backdoor slider on the outside half of the plate. Gibson reached out, connected, and like something out of *The Natural,* the ball flew into the right-field stands, a two-run homer to win the game. All Eckersley could do was helplessly watch one of the most theatrical home runs ever, and then slowly walk off the field with the crowd's maddening din ringing in his ears.

The incredible roll that Eckersley was on in 1988—the forty-five saves in the regular season and the record four saves against Boston in the playoffs—had finally come to a halt. His wife, Nancy, who had cried for happiness in the stands when he beat his former team, the Red Sox, then took the emotional plunge. "When I saw the home run," she said, "I just cringed. I thought, 'Oh, my God.' "

Her husband was a recovering alcoholic, and in former days the old "Eck as in Wreck" would surely have gotten dead drunk. That night in Los Angeles, Eckersley had dinner, and outwardly kept an even keel, but he couldn't sleep, and in fact it took him a few months to get over it. There were even nightmares, deftly edited—Eckersley has a ball in his hand, a scruffy-looking batter limps to the plate. "I never got a good look at the face. I assume it was him. In the dreams, though, he popped up a few times."

His honesty about how the home run tormented him is rare in the sport, and especially rare for the closer, who is often a flake or super-macho character who acts as if nothing affects him. But Eckersley gets tight every time he takes the mound with a game on the line. He describes the job of the closer as "pure stress." By the fifth inning he'll have a cigarette to help him go to the bathroom, so he doesn't have to while he's warming up in the bullpen.

Once he's in the game, he works fast, anxious to end things. "Baseball is not *fun*," he insists, "until it's all over." Yet Eckersley has become addicted to the pressure. When he was on the disabled list with a rotator cuff problem in 1989, he found himself actually missing the stress of relieving, longing for those agonizing minutes when his stomach ties itself in knots. "Isn't it sick, missing this shit?" he once told me. "I say it while I'm doing it. 'I like this shit? What am I, fucking crazy!?' " Eckersley had come back too far from his years of dissolution for the Gibson homer to derail him. In 1989, hungrier than ever, he closed out a world championship for the A's.

Moore's death does indeed have some precedent in baseball. Seventy-seven major league ballplayers have committed suicide. Almost half of them were pitchers, an indication of the kind of pressure that goes with this unique position in sports. One of the most hellish moments for a pitcher in the history of the game came in 1941, the Dodgers-Yankees World Series.

The Series was even at a game apiece going into the third game, and Fred Fitzsimmons, at forty the oldest pitcher ever to start in a World Series, was throwing shutout ball for seven innings; the game was in fact scoreless. But the final out of the seventh inning was a line drive that hit Fitzie square on the kneecap, knocking him out of the game.

Manager Leo Durocher summoned Hugh Casey to hold the Yanks in the eighth, and the Yankees got four hits and scored two runs. Two plays made Casey look bad. One was a routine grounder on which Casey failed to cover first base. The other was when he again stood immobile on the mound when he had Red Rolfe, who had gotten the first hit, picked cleanly off second. Durocher asked him about that play after the game. Casey said, "I don't know what happened to me, Skip. I wanted to throw the ball but I just froze."

The next day it looked like the Dodgers would tie up the Series again, as they led 4–3 going into the ninth inning. Casey had all but redeemed himself, coming into the game in the fifth inning and retiring Joe Gordon with the bases loaded. He breezed through the powerful Yanks until he got the first two batters out in the ninth inning. Then he had two strikes on Tommy Henrich. Now Casey threw a hard sinker that Henrich swung at and missed by a foot. Strike three. The game was over. Uh-uh. As the umpire yelled "Strike three," Henrich turned around and saw the ball had gotten by Owen, and Tommy scrambled to first base.

Like Rich Gedman failing to catch Bob Stanley's sinker in Game Six of the '86 World Series, Mickey Owen had failed to shift his feet, stabbing at the ball instead. The pitch tipped off the end of Owen's glove and didn't roll at all that far behind the catcher, but it was far enough. And the Yankees were alive.

There was still only a man on first with two out. Time to take a deep breath, regroup, and mass every ounce of strength and concentration together. But Casey pitched to DiMaggio almost as soon as he had the ball in his hand, and Joe D. hit a bullet into left field, Henrich racing to third. The next batter was the left-handed Charlie Keller.

Durocher watched from the dugout, unable, somehow, to make any kind of move. "Given everything that had been happening, the situation screamed for me to replace Casey with [lefty reliever Larry] French," he recalled later. "I did nothing. I froze. Casey slowed himself down, made two good pitches, and once again we were only one strike away. I had a thought of going out to remind him to brush Keller back with the next pitch. Maybe even the next two pitches."

He didn't, and then watched in horror as his pitcher grooved a room-service fastball to the dangerous Keller. King Kong, as he was called, doubled against the wall in right, scoring Henrich and Di-Maggio, and the Yankees won the game and then the Series.

The freewheeling, hard-drinking Casey rebounded from the failure of nerve in that traumatic Series, and had some more good seasons before serving his country in World War II. But some years after he retired from baseball, in 1951, he shot himself in the head. At the time he was trying to get back with his wife, whom he was crazy about, when he was slapped with a paternity suit by a woman described by several ballplayers as a baseball groupie. He was talking on the phone with his wife, and when she said she wouldn't come back to him, he put a gun in his mouth and pulled the trigger.

"I know that he had all the guts in the world," Durocher said of Casey. But once upon a time, he came up short. Pressure can be a funny thing. It's not the weaklings who can be driven to distraction by the pressure. Sometimes you have to play games with yourself, another game within the game that has nothing and everything to do with baseball.

Think of Goose Gossage on the mound in the '78 playoff game between the Yankees and the Red Sox. He faced Carl Yastrzemski in the bottom of the ninth inning with the tying run on third, and the winning run on first. Yaz had homered earlier in the game against twenty-five-game winner Ron Guidry. All of a sudden Gossage didn't think he could throw the next pitch. But he thought to himself, "The worst thing that could happen if we lose is that at this time tomorrow I'll be skiing in the Rockies." He regained control of himself and fired the exploding fastball that Yastrzemski popped up for the final out.

Another one who faced plenty of these do-or-die situations was Tug McGraw. He developed something he called "the frozen iceball theory of pitching." "If I come in to pitch with the bases loaded and Willie Stargell at bat, there's no rational reason I would want to throw the ball. As long as I hold onto it, nothing bad can happen. But I'm aware that eventually I have to pitch. So what I do is remind myself that in approximately a billion years the sun is going to burn out and the earth will become a frozen iceball hurtling through space. And when that happens, nobody's going to care what Willie Stargell did with the bases loaded."

Tell that to Ralph Branca, who gave up the "shot heard 'round the world" in 1951. The unfortunate pitcher who wore number thirteen on that day lives with the moment still. The Dodgers had held a thirteen-and-one-half-game lead over the Giants as late as August, when the Giants began an incredible run, winning thirty-seven of their last forty-four games. The two teams were tied at the end of the regular season, and a best-of-three playoff began for the National League pennant.

It came down to the final game, in which Don Newcombe was pitching for the Dodgers. He was removed from the game in the ninth inning with a 4–2 lead, two men on and two out. Bobby Thomson was at the plate. In the Dodgers bullpen, two pitchers were throwing, Branca and Carl Erskine. When the call came from manager Charlie Dressen to bullpen coach Clyde Sukeforth, Erskine was bouncing his curve in front of the catcher, and Sukeforth reported it. "Give me Branca," said Dressen.

Branca had pitched the first playoff game at Ebbets Field, and lost. In fact, Bobby Thomson had homered off him in that game. When he started to warm up earlier in the third game, he could barely throw the ball fifty feet. He rubbed some hot stuff called Capsulin on his arm, and finally his stiff arm loosened up enough in the ninth so he could pitch. Dressen gave him the ball with this strategic command: "Get him out."

From the third-base coaching box, Durocher called Thomson over and asked him what pitch he hit for the homer off Branca in the first game. "Was it a slider?" he asked. Thomson didn't remember that it was actually a fastball, so he said it was a slider. "Then look for a fastball this time," Leo said. "He remembers you hit a slider. He won't throw it again. Just be ready for the fastball."

The first pitch was right down the pipe, a fastball in a hittable zone. Thomson later acknowledged that it was a meatball, and didn't know why he took it for strike one. Durocher hollered down to Thomson, "C'mon, now, he'll come back with one." Campanella was not catching because of an injury, and catcher Rube Walker just threw the ball back to Branca, instead of doing what some think Campy would have done—gone out to the mound and chewed out Branca for throwing a pitch so juicy in that situation. Branca threw another fastball, and Thomson was ready for it.

Years later, Branca answered the question of what he was thinking about. "The next pitch I had wanted to waste, so I threw a fastball up and in, and I might have aimed it, which I tend to believe I probably did, and he hit it with an uppercut, it had overspin, and he hit it down the line, and it was sinking and all I could remember saying was 'Sink, sink, sink,' and it just did go in. It went in like six inches over the wall. Probably went over the wall at 300 feet."

Many years later, Branca went to dinner with Sal Maglie, the Giants pitcher, who asked, "If you were trying to waste the pitch 'cause you wanted him to hit the curveball, why didn't you just throw him the curveball?" Or, someone else asked, why didn't he just brush Thomson back with the fastball? There were a million questions, a million "What ifs?"

Ralph Branca won twenty games in a season when he was twenty-one years old, and not many other pitchers have done that, but he's remembered only for the home-run ball he threw that decided the '51 pennant. How many times has the famous call of the game on radio by Russ Hodges been replayed, in his hoarse disbelieving refrain?: "The Giants win the pennant!"

As an insurance salesman, Branca often finds himself talking about the home run. But he tries not to mind it too much. "I'm immune by now," he said forty years later. One thing that did bother him happened when the New York Mets released a photo of Branca in an advertisement emphasizing great moments in New York baseball.

It was a blown-up picture of the stricken young pitcher, sobbing into his hands. The Mets pulled the ad when they found out that Branca was not happy about it.

"I've lived with this thing for forty years," he said. "It's about time it died." At one point, years ago, Branca was so troubled that he asked a priest, "Father, why did this have to happen to me?" And the priest told him, "God gave you this cross to bear because he knew you'd be strong enough to carry it."

Dingers and Brushbacks

Something special happens when a batter hits a home run, some perfect combination of bat angle and speed. Only about one-sixteenth of an inch separates a line drive single from a lofty, soaring home run. But that's a yawning gap and so when the home run is struck, it does something to the hitters, galvanizes their imagination, for one. That's why they tend to give their long balls nicknames—the tater, the dinger, the tonk, the Big Fly—the celebration of the home run.

How a batter reacts after hitting a home run had not changed very much from the time of Babe Ruth to the October day, thirty-four years later, in 1961 when Roger Maris broke the Babe's record. It went this way: the hitter circling the bases with his head down, then shaking hands briefly with the third-base coach, then the next hitter and the batboy—all without breaking stride. That's how Maris did it; when he hit a game-winning home run, his eyes would be down at the ground, stolidly ignoring the storm of adulation around him. Even when he hit number sixty-one, his teammates had to push him out of the dugout to take a curtain call.

Some players, of course, developed a signature home run trot, but departure from the norm was a rarity. There was the time when Jim Piersall ran around the bases backwards after hitting his hundredth career home run off Dallas Green in New York. That was then. Today, we have fifty-seven varieties of homer salutations—the High Five, the Low Five, the Double High Five, the Elbow Bash popularized by the Oakland A's, and the Dual Shoulder Smack, a Bo Jackson innovation. Nobody wanted to get put on the disabled list for two months, however, just because Bo hit a homer. (Back in 1985, the Dodgers' Steve Sax homered and romped excitedly around the bases. When he arrived at third, he gave coach Joe Amalfitano such a thunderous high-five that he broke Amalfitano's thumb.)

Few pitchers really admire the long home runs that they gave up, Hall of Famer Catfish Hunter being one exception. Hunter was especially fond of the homers that, in his words, "brought rain." Pitchers do tend to remember the tape-measure shots. While hitters like to express the cliché "I know a ball is gone the moment it's hit," some go even further. Hall of Famer Fergie Jenkins remembered a ball he threw to Willie McCovey. "It was a low curveball and as soon as I released the pitch I thought, 'Well, at least there's nobody on base.' He crushed it. It went over the players' parking lot behind the stadium and halfway into the attendants' parking lot before it bounced. It's probably still floating in the [San Francisco] bay somewhere."

One thing that makes a pitcher really do a fast burn is when the batter tries to intimidate the pitcher with his menacing preparations at the plate. The most famous such incident was of course the controversial "called shot" by Babe Ruth in the 1932 World Series. As the legend goes, Ruth, with two strikes and two balls on him, stepped out of the box, and then gestured majestically with his bat toward the center-field bleachers. Cubs pitcher Charlie Root, seemingly transfixed by the Ruthian gesture, threw one down the middle and Ruth poleaxed the ball high and deep to precisely the spot he had pointed toward. Did it really happen that way? Some observers said yes, some said no. Never mind: the "called shot" remained an integral part of Ruthian mythology.

In the pitiful Hollywood film version of Ruth's life starring the terminally uncoordinated William Bendix, the legend was taken as an absolute fact. This enraged Charlie Root, who turned down the opportunity to portray himself in the movie. Root went to his grave denying that Ruth had pointed to center field. "If he had I would have knocked him on his ass with the next pitch," he insisted.

In the summer of 1988, an Illinois man turned up saying that he had film footage from the game in question. Upon hearing of the find, adrenaline flowed in the veins of excited baseball historians everywhere. It was baseball's equivalent of the Zapruder home movie of John Kennedy's assassination, and the buffs couldn't wait to get their hands on it.

But after the archivists watched the film, they couldn't see Ruth calling the shot. The amateur cinematographer was aghast. "Didn't you see him point?" he said. Upon closer scrutiny, it did seem that Ruth, after drawing his bat back, had taken one hand off the bat and pointed with his forefinger, with a little pistol movement, *twice,* just before the fateful pitch came in to him. One can now say with some certainty that he either did or did not point to the bleachers. The legend lives on.

What would be the pitcher's version of the called shot? Probably something like Satchel Paige did when he reacted to a particularly vivid racial slur during a barnstorming tour. Paige called in his fielders with the bases loaded and no outs and proceeded to strike out the side. But the poor pitcher who gives up a big home run at the wrong time has to stay on the mound and take it. Pitchers who hate home runs, and that covers the entire fraternity, try not to watch the hitter circle the bases. Instead they keep their backs to the runner as he trots around the bases. Some just hold out their gloves for a new ball from the umpire. "Once after I'd given up another home run," said former Indians pitcher and Royals pitching coach Frank Funk, "I stood out there thinking, 'Now I know why the umpire doesn't give me a new baseball until that hitter crosses home plate—he knows that if he gave it to me too soon I'd nail that hitter with it when he came around third base.' "

One thing the pitcher can do is take out his anger on the next batter. It happens a lot in baseball. Luis Tiant never understood the logic behind the move. "Somebody hit a home run, I don't throw at the next guy. What does that fuckin' guy have to do with it? I think that's chickenshit."

The beanball pitch remains the most lethal weapon in the pitcher's arsenal when it comes to facing a dangerous batter. Although few ballplayers like to talk about it openly, fear is quite simply one of the fundamental, basic features of facing fast pitching. If a hardball should hit any part of the batter's body, it will certainly hurt; if it hits certain vulnerable areas, like elbows, wrists, or face, it can cause broken bones and other serious injuries; and if it hits a particular area of an unprotected head, it can kill. Nobody can play professionally who hasn't mastered his fear.

"I remember as a kid around the playgrounds in California," said Ted Williams, "hearing the guys talking about beanballs, about scaring the batters, brushing them back, making them dance. I made up my mind way back then, 'They aren't going to scare me.' " In all sports, the athlete has to perform knowing the possibility of getting hurt; awareness of the fear is pushed aside. But on some instinctive level, the batter is afraid, and how he hits in spite of this fear is the measure of his success. "As far as the fear hitters have of getting conked with the ball," said Williams, "all hitters go through it, and they must accept terror as a pitcher's legitimate weapon. A pitcher puts a hitter through those test periods. Start wearing down the fences and they start giving you a look, and then they find out if you can hit from the prone position."

After he retired from the game, Ken "Hawk" Harrelson freely talked about the fear factor. "I played nine years in the majors scared to death. I've seen great players who were intimidated at the plate in certain situations, and anybody who's been around this game for long has seen pitchers who made fear part of their repertoire."

It is one of the tenets of the game that a pitcher must throw inside to win. "Show me a guy," said Don Drysdale, "who can't pitch inside and I'll show you a loser." A pitcher must gain the respect of hitters who are digging in with their spikes for maximum leverage and diving in to slam his pitches. No hitter begrudges the pitcher the right to try and win that respect by driving the hitter off the plate. At the same time, the hitter can't give in either. As Al Kaline said, "Show me a hitter who can't be jammed and I'll show you a horseshit hitter."

If you play major league baseball long enough, and you don't bat with your keister in the dugout, then eventually you are going to not only get hit by a pitch, but beaned in the head. Frank Robinson was a veteran of the beanball wars. Robinson was hit by pitches twenty times in his rookie year, which easily led the league. He continued to lead the league in each of his ten National League seasons.

Robinson said he stood as close to the plate as he could and stuck his head out over it, right in the middle of what they call "concussion alley," so that he could get the best possible view of the ball when it left the pitcher's hand. He also liked being able to hit the ball away from him with power. Robinson had his preferred method of handling a ball that was coming into him. "Tuck your head into your shoulder and spin left. Quickly. If the pitch was too far inside, you spun and fell hard away from it. So a pitcher would knock me down, and I'd get right back up and hang over the plate again."

The brushback pitch is protected by a covenant between pitchers and hitters that is baseball's open secret. *I'm coming inside. Get your ass out of the way. But I'm not going for the head.* It's only when a brushback pitch is aimed behind the head that it becomes a blatant beanball, and a potentially deadly pitch. Pitchers deny ever throwing this kind of pitch; they always say that the ball just got away from them or ran or sailed. But the beanball is sometimes used to send a stronger message than the brushback.

In the 1980 World Series, the Kansas City Royals were swinging hot bats and dominating play. George Brett, in particular, was having an exceptional Series. The Philadelphia Phillies brought in Dickie Noles, and he promptly threw behind Brett's head, turning him upside down in the batter's box. Brett narrowly escaped a serious beaning, there was a little rhubarb on the field, and then Brett, and the entire Royals team, stopped hitting. After the Phillies won the championship, it was hard not to look back at that beanball incident as the turning point of the Series.

Nobody can read the mind of a pitcher and know what motivated him to throw to a certain location. Early Wynn, a 300-game winner, was once accused of being mean enough to throw at his own grandmother, but he denied it. "Only if she was digging in," he said. Pitchers can joke about it all they want, but any time a pitcher tries to brush a hitter back, there is a danger that the pitch can miss by a foot or two and hit the batter in the head.

That is why some pitchers, especially the ones who throw really hard, are sometimes afraid to throw inside because they themselves fear really hurting somebody. The great Walter Johnson played the game this way, and that's why Ty Cobb hit him so well during their long careers—he knew Johnson wouldn't brush him back. In a 1912 game against the Yankees, Johnson hit a player named Jack Martin in the cheek with a fastball. At the time he was leading 7–0. Johnson got so upset that he lost the game 8–7.

Two of the most wondrous fastball pitchers of the modern era, Sandy Koufax and Nolan Ryan, always pitched inside but absolutely would not throw at hitters. The fear of maiming batters may be at the root of Steve Dalkowski's failure to make it as a big-league pitcher. Despite being only five-foot-eight, this left-hander could regularly throw his fastball 110 miles per hour, but he could also walk twenty men in a single game. Former Red Sox catcher Bob Montgomery thought the reason Dalkowski was so wild was "he was afraid he was going to kill somebody."

Other pitchers, right from the get-go, feel they have to be intimidating to be successful. Mike Harkey was the Chicago Cubs' number-one pitching prospect when he first pitched in the majors in September of 1988, not the least reason being his ninety-plus mph fastball. He's six five, and likes to glower in at the hitters with that baleful stare that Nolan Ryan perfected over the last twenty years. But some scouts had openly questioned Harkey's intestinal fortitude. So Harkey wanted to demonstrate that he had what it takes right away when he came up to the Cubs. The first major league hitter that Harkey faced was the dangerous stud-in-the-clutch, Pedro Guerrero. Harkey hit him in the head to announce his entry into the major leagues. After losing the '89 season because of a serious knee injury, he established himself the following year as one of the most intimidating and successful young pitchers in the game. Through 1990, Harkey was hitting batters at Don Drysdale's career ratio: one out of every twenty-two hitters he faced.

Although there have been several beanball deaths in the minor leagues, it is something of a wonder that only one player has been killed by a beanball in the history of the majors. In 1920 Carl Mays of the New York Yankees was one of the best control pitchers in baseball. But he also led the league in hit batsmen. While Walter

Johnson wouldn't throw at Ty Cobb, Mays wantonly terrorized Cobb, befitting his personality profile as an egotistical S.O.B. who gave no quarter. Cobb tried to get his revenge by bunting down the first-base line and running over Mays with his spikes. But in his next at-bat, Mays just decked Cobb again . . . twice.

In August 1920, the Yankees faced the Cleveland Indians, with both teams neck and neck in a tough pennant race. Carl Mays was the Yankees' ace, on his way to a twenty-six-win season, and was giving the Indians fits with his submarine deliveries. The game was scoreless when Ray Chapman came up to start the fifth inning. Chapman was hitting .303 at the time and had already scored ninety-seven runs that season. Mays threw a fastball that swooped inside to the batter, who made no effort to move. The ball crashed against his unprotected left temple (batters wore no helmets in those days). Mays heard the noise, then saw the ball bouncing back toward him. Thinking it had struck the bat handle, he grabbed it and threw to first base. Only when Mays saw first baseman Wally Pipp looking at home plate, frozen with the ball held above his head, did he realize something was wrong.

Chapman died a day later after surgery could not relieve pressure on his brain. For a week, Mays had to go into hiding. He returned to pitch only home games because fan reaction to him was so antagonistic. *The Sporting News* wrote that if players were told a hitter had been killed by a pitch and not told who threw it, they would have guessed it was Mays. Some teams threatened to boycott Mays after the incident, though no one followed through.

Although Mays was known as a pitcher who intentionally threw at batters, the beaning itself was accidental insofar as it was almost certainly produced by the combination of a dirty ball moving inside and Chapman's inability to see the pitch on a gray, drizzly day. So he froze at the plate. At that time, teams did not use clean, new balls. The typical pre-1921 baseball was a grimy object, covered with players' spit, licorice, and tobacco juice, which turned it more black than white. After this shocking death, the owners banned spitballs and agreed that new, clean, more easily visible balls should be used routinely. Pitchers, of course, were furious with the changes, and batters hit more homers as balls traveled farther and faster. Period-ically, the game has enforced the intimidation of hitters in varying degrees, and the number of beanballs and hit batters has in fact risen and fallen in different periods.

In the '50s and '60s, the brushback pitch again became routine, possibly because leading pitchers of that era based their careers on intimidation. Two such pitchers flourished in the National League at that time—Don Drysdale and Bob Gibson. When Mickey Mantle was asked who the toughest pitchers were that he faced in his career, he said it was between Drysdale and Koufax, "but Koufax didn't try to hit you with the ball."

Drysdale, before a game, would often ask hitters where they wanted to be hit, and then after hitting them he would ask them if they wanted him to autograph the bruise. One night before an All-Star Game he sat around in a bar with some American League hitters until very late, and all of a sudden started laughing. His fellow All-Star drinking companions thought he was in his cups, until he was able to compose himself and explain his merriment: "You guys probably think I'm not gonna try and hit you tomorrow."

Drysdale used simple arithmetic when his own team was being thrown at. "If one of our guys went down, then two of theirs would go down. If two of our guys went down, then four of theirs went down. I just doubled it." One time he was trying to hit opposing pitcher Dick "Turk" Farrell, a former Phillie and original Colt .45, because of some old vendetta, but he walked him instead. Farrell got to second base and Drysdale drilled him in the side with a pickoff throw. Like the Canadian Mounties, Drysdale always got his man.

Bob Gibson was a different sort from Drysdale, deadly serious about his profession. Gibson didn't like to fraternize with any opponents; he didn't want to learn about their families or anything that would humanize them. At the All-Star Game, he wouldn't talk to any of his teammates because he knew that in a few days they would go back to being his mortal enemies, and that's the way he approached his job.

Gibson looked at hitters as people who were literally trying to take the food out of his children's mouths, and pitched accordingly. He fully acknowledged the deep animosity that can fester between hitters and pitchers. Sentiment just didn't enter into it. Gibson roomed with first baseman Bill White of the Cardinals for years, but as soon as White was traded to the Phillies, Gibson plunked him with a fastball the first time he pitched against him.

"Even before Bill was traded," Gibson explained, "I used to tell him that if he ever dived across the plate to swing at an outside pitch, the way he liked to, I'd have to hit him. And then, the very first time, he went for a pitch that was *this* far outside and swung at it, and so I hit him on the elbow with the next pitch. Bill saw it coming, and he yelled 'Yaah!' even before it got him. And I yelled over to him, 'You son of a bitch, you went for that outside ball! That pitch, that part of the plate, belongs to *me*! If I make a mistake inside, all right, but the outside is mine and don't you forget it.' He said, 'You're crazy,' but he understood me."

Gibson's out pitch was down and away, and it was obviously much more difficult to hit if the batter had to anticipate an inside pitch. "There were some players that all the pitchers knew about," acknowledged Gibson, "guys you could throw at early in the game and then not worry about them hurting you later."

And then there were hitters that most pitchers didn't throw at, because they had proved they could get up and take you deep. Prime examples were Reggie Jackson and Frank Robinson. When the hard throwers gave up throwing at the head, they were not just showing respect; they were paying a kind of ultimate compliment. Some pitchers, however, never agreed to a cease-fire. If, for instance, any hitter dug his spikes in and got too comfortable when Stan Williams was pitching, he would step off the mound and say, "That's a nice hole you're digging. Make it at least six feet deep, because you're going to be buried in it."

Williams, the Reds' pitching coach in the year of their 1990 world championship, presided over the bullpen of Norm Charlton, Rob Dibble, and Randy Myers, known as "The Nasty Boys." All three could throw ninety-five mph heat, and were known for making hitters uncomfortable and not apologizing for it. Williams himself did apologize one time. After he dazed Hank Aaron by hitting him in the helmet with a fastball, he said he was sorry: "I meant to hit you in the neck!" he explained. Williams used to keep a picture of Aaron hanging near his locker so he could throw at it to keep game-sharp.

All of the Reds' relievers were intimidators because of their sheer speed. Rob Dibble in particular, who has registered one hundred mph on radar guns, has been involved in more than his share of flaps, earning several league fines and suspensions for throwing at hitters. He claims, however, that while his fastball is wicked, his reputation is undeserved. "I've been called a headhunter, a lot of things. But I don't play games with people's careers. I'm a big believer that there's enough money in this game for a lot of people to be happy for many years. Why would I hit a guy and risk something like what happened to Dickie Thon or Conigliaro? I remember things like that. Me being a guy capable of ending someone's life and being a Christian, I'm not that type of person." And yet when the Expos' Tom Foley said that Dibble was becoming the most disliked player in the league, Dibble noted that Foley has to hit off him and was taking "a hell of a risk saying something like that."

The threat of the brushback pitch works different ways on different people. Don Baylor got hit over two hundred times and it didn't change his approach. Baylor would never rub himself when he got hit. He was just one of those ballplayers who could wait comfortably for a fastball to drill him in the arm or shoulder or side.

Hank Greenberg said that he never saw Lou Gehrig move away from an inside pitch—the "Iron Horse" would just jerk his chin back without moving his body, without ever giving in. This would infuriate pitchers, of course. Carl Yastrzemski had the same talent, so he really didn't mind very much if the pitch was right at his head; what really bothered him was getting hit in the elbow, wrist, or legs. When Darrell Evans was pitched inside, instead of backing off the plate he would just try to pull those pitches inside the foul pole. "I never got hit," he said. "Maybe twice a year. I didn't think about it. Whenever you think about it, you slow down. So I never thought about it." Ron Hunt, the Mets' second baseman in the '60s, actually *tried* to get hit. It was part of his game, to get on base by having the ball hit him in the rear end, or, his specialty, have the ball just brush his billowy uniform sleeves.

Managers used to fine pitchers if they didn't hit a certain guy. Sometimes they would give a signal on the bench, holding a finger up to their ear. It meant "stick it in his ear." Leo Durocher loved to do this when he was managing and let the other team see it, too. Opposing teams were always protesting the tactics of Durocher-led ball clubs, claiming that he goaded the whole staff into becoming beanball artists.

Earl Weaver, on the other hand, would not allow his pitchers to throw at a batter. Umpires never had to warn Orioles pitchers about beanballs, and the long list of Baltimore twenty-game winners is proof that pitchers can win without the beanball. Weaver felt, as many do, that "Stick it in his ear" is an ugly and immoral order to send down on a ballfield, because it means not just to throw *at* the batter's head but to throw just *behind* the batter's head.

By obeying the natural instinct of ducking one's head backwards from a pitch, the batter can easily be badly beaned by a pitch behind his head, at the risk of concussion or permanent brain-scrambling. Don Zimmer wears a steel plate in his head because of such a brush-back-that-became-a-beanball. It is one thing to be an intimidating brushback pitcher, and another to try intentionally to split a batter's helmet, and pitchers are eager to make the distinction. "When I threw at a guy, I hit him," said Gibson. "But I never threw at a guy's head."

For years, the balance of power between the hitter and the pitcher was kept by a variation of Hammurabi's Code of an eye for an eye and a tooth for a tooth, as the pitchers, with their threat of retaliation, generally kept the game from becoming a bean-brawl. But this long-standing tradition of accepted terrorizing of hitters changed when the Players Association was formed in the early '70s. As Carl Yastrzemski said, "It was as if you didn't want to hurt your fellow union member. Nobody threw at you anymore. It became very comfortable getting into that batter's box and hitting."

Several new rules had a big effect as well. For one thing, the designated-hitter rule in the American League eliminated the pitcher coming up to bat, so there was no revenge to be gotten by throwing at him. Also important was the new rule instituted whereby the umpire, after the first brushback pitch, would issue a warning to the pitcher. Any close pitch from either side from then on could be cause for ejection from the game. So the pitchers couldn't retaliate in the next half inning anymore, and the hitters began getting comfortable at the plate after the warning, waggling their backsides and getting ready to dive right into the ball with a hearty swing from their heels. But the new rule has its downside. On the one hand, it gives one team an initial free brushback, with no fear of retaliation. So, after a warning is issued, the batters get a free ride, and what pitchers do to offset this advantage to the hitter is to throw inside anyway. And lots of times the hitters aren't ready. This is what happened to Andre Dawson when he was in a hot streak, diving into pitches. He simply wasn't ready for an inside pitch, and got hit in the face by Eric Show of the Padres.

The attempt to tame the game has also made it commonplace for the hitter to take matters into his own hands. Since he cannot rely on his own pitcher to retaliate for him, he charges the mound. When this happens, the hitter only has three seconds before five guys from the other team will be on top of him, so the fans are frequently treated to a poor imitation of a kung-fu movie, as the enraged batter now flashes karate kicks at the offending pitcher. This is what George Bell tried to do to Bruce Kison in one of those three-second melees. Others react differently. Once Pedro Guerrero got hit with a curveball from David Cone in Los Angeles and disdainfully threw his bat toward the mound, earning a suspension for himself.

Juan Marichal once attacked Dodger catcher John Roseboro with a bat, which probably kept him out of the Hall of Fame for years after he should have been voted in on the merits of his outstanding career. Marichal was batting in a less-than-agreeable Dodger-Giant game and Roseboro was throwing the ball back to his pitcher so that Marichal could hear it whizzing past his ear, making him one of the few hitters to go bananas because he was being brushed back by the catcher.

Frank Robinson had a little scare in his second major league season when Ruben Gomez of the then New York Giants hit him in the head and cracked his helmet, sending him to the hospital for X rays. He played the next day and went on to have another good year. But in 1958 he was hit by Camilo Pascual of the Washington Senators during an exhibition game, and this time woke up in the hospital. Robinson was put in an ambulance and driven to Cincinnati. "It was

120 miles away on a bumpy road, and my head felt every bump. I had a cerebral concussion, but there was no fracture."

When the '58 season opened, Robinson played even though he had constant headaches, and worse, was simply scared to death when he tried to hit, and couldn't stop pulling away from the pitch. "The fear in my subconscious was excruciating. Fear was going to drive me out of the game. I either had to conquer my fear or find another line of work." In the midst of this crisis, he faced the pitcher who had fractured his helmet, Ruben Gomez, and forced himself to hang in. "He tried to back me off the plate with an inside fastball, and I lined it to left. Then I felt my confidence was all the way back. For the next eight years, I never had a problem with fear of striding into pitches."

Chris Brown was at one time one of the most promising young players in the big leagues, an All-Star third baseman with the Giants in 1986 at the age of twenty-four. He was later traded to San Diego, and then released by Detroit and Pittsburgh, unable to hit .250 in the big leagues since his banner year. Many have questioned his attitude and willingness to play, but it didn't help when a pitch from Danny Cox in St. Louis in 1987 broke his jaw and knocked him unconscious for a few seconds.

When Brown came back six weeks later, he was tentative at the plate, and the pitchers took advantage of it. "After I got hit and tried to come back, pitchers kept testing me, knocking me down," he said. "That's how they make their living; I understand that. But there were times I'd be down in the dirt, and I'd have flashbacks to that pitch that hit me."

In baseball tragedy is never more than a pitch away. One of baseball's saddest stories ended in 1990 with the death of Tony Conigliaro at the age of forty-five. He came up with the Red Sox in 1964, and some veteran observers called him the best-looking young hitter they had ever seen. He became the youngest major league player to hit one hundred career home runs. And then in 1967 he was hit on the left side of his face by a pitch from California's Jack Hamilton, a pitch that got away from the usually mild-mannered pitcher. It fractured Conigliaro's cheekbone, dislocated his jaw, and badly blurred his vision. Dick Dew, a sportswriter covering the game, said the sound of ball impacting on face stopped everybody in the park. "It was unmistakable," he said. "You knew the injury was serious the moment you heard it."

Conigliaro sat out that season and the next, and doctors gave him little chance of being able to hit again, but he found that if he turned his head just a bit toward the pitcher, he could still see a pitched ball well enough to hit it. Conigliaro returned in 1969 and won the Comeback Player of the Year award. The following year, he had career highs of thirty-six home runs and 116 runs batted in. But in 1971 he was traded to California, and didn't finish the season; his vision had deteriorated badly. A 1975 comeback with the Red Sox ended after only twenty-one games, and again, as in 1967, the year of the beaning, Boston went on to the World Series without "Tony C," who was still only thirty years old.

After kicking around as a television sports broadcaster for a few years, in 1982 he auditioned to be the television announcer for the Red Sox and got the job. His brother Billy, who also played for Boston, was driving him to Logan Airport so he could fly back to San Francisco, where he was living, and then come home to what looked like, finally, some good luck. But in the car Tony suffered a serious heart attack, and for five minutes his heart stopped. For a time, Tony Conigliaro was clinically dead, his brain was damaged, and he was in a coma for four months. He never recovered from it, requiring constant care and frequent hospitalization until his death.

Orioles center fielder Paul Blair had his own flirtation with disaster in 1970 when he was hit just below the helmet by a fastball from California Angels pitcher Ken Tatum. He went down as if shot, and blood trickled out of his nose, mouth, and ears. Sometimes it can take years for a player to recover from a serious beaning. After Dickie Thon was hit in the eye by Mike Torrez in 1984, it was five years before he was a regular again in the majors, and he didn't come close to his All-Star numbers before the accident. In Blair's case, even though every bone on the left side of his face was broken, he missed only twenty-one days before he returned to playing.

"Had I seen the ball coming in," Blair recalled, "it might have had an effect on me as far as coming back. But I never saw it because I was looking for something else. I had faced Ken Tatum in winter ball in Puerto Rico and he always started me off with the slider. I was hot at the time, I had just hit three home runs in a game, I was two for three in that ballgame and I was looking to hit that slider out of the ballpark. He threw me an inside fastball and I never saw it. I was just concentrating on something else. If I would have seen it, I could have gotten out of the way, because up to that point I had never been hit in the head. I always prided myself on the fact that nobody could hit me in the head, my reactions were so quick.

"When they had a panel on 'Nightline' about beanballs, my suggestion about what they should do was this—if a pitcher hit a batter in the head, and the batter was hurt, the pitcher should stay out as long as the batter was out. There is no reason for a pitcher to hit a batter in the head—if you want to send a message you can hit him in the ribs, and you still can intimidate people. But if you hit somebody in the head, you're messing with their *life,* not just their livelihood."

Pity the Poor Hitter

Does anyone think there is anything more difficult in sports than hitting a baseball? All a batter has to do is swat at a sphere three inches in diameter with a piece of slim rounded wood. Geometrically speaking, one must connect almost perfectly to get a base hit; a line drive can only result if the line from the center of the ball through the point of impact to the very center of the bat is almost perfectly straight. The area in which the bat and ball can meet squarely like this is not more than half an inch.

Ray Miller, pitching coach of the Pirates, is not alone when he says he doesn't understand how anyone can hit. "It's hard enough to hit a golf ball," he said, "and it's not even moving." An eighty-five-mph pitch comes in from the pitcher's hand to home plate in a little less than half a second, so the batter has about a quarter of a second to decide where to swing. When put this way, hitting seems close to impossible, like eating soup with a fork or dialing phone numbers with your feet. The batter is able to accomplish the impossible because hitting becomes a trained reflex honed by hundreds of thousands of swings.

All of us who've played the game for fun know how difficult it is to hit any kind of decent pitching. As a ten-year-old, I used to have a fantasy derived from the old Colgate toothpaste commercials, which featured fastball pitchers like Don Drysdale throwing against a see-through Indestructible Shield, which was supposed to symbolize protection against tooth decay. That's the only way I ever wanted to try hitting against major league pitchers, safe behind the Colgate Shield.

There are daredevil fans who would like the opportunity to turn around a fastball from one of the real flamethrowers—Nolan Ryan or Roger Clemens. I watched pitchers like this warm up from very close range when they were throwing in the nineties, just getting loose really, and I would tell these guys, "Believe me, you don't want to hit against pitchers like this, even with a lot of padding and a regulation pith helmet. In fact, I don't think you really want to play catch with them, either."

The real trick with the great fastball pitchers is controlling the heater. Early in his career, Sandy Koufax had a terrible problem with his control. Even after he got to the majors, he used to play catch and throw half the balls over his partner's head. But his coaches finally discovered the secret of Koufax's wildness: that in reaching back and trying to put everything he had into every pitch, he was creating too much muscular tension. A little rocking motion put rhythm into his delivery. "He needed a loose wrist," said Dodger pitching coach Joe Beckwith, "to get snap in the ball at the position of release." Koufax soon realized that less was more, that by throwing more easily the ball would not only travel as fast but would go where he wanted it to.

"All at once Sandy got control," Walter Alston said. "And I don't mean control in the sense of just throwing the ball over the plate. He could throw the fastball where he wanted to—to spots. When you have that kind of stuff and that kind of control, well, they just stopped hitting him. And it all happened in one year. It made me a much smarter manager."

Another one who had to overcome wildness was Nolan Ryan. As a young gun in the Met organization, Ryan was never sure where his pitches were going. But after his trade to the Angels, he established control of a sharp-breaking curve as well as his fastball. He even pitched his fifth no-hitter (Ryan has thrown seven, the all-time record) against the Dodgers by relying on the curve, since he didn't have his overpowering fastball on that occasion.

At forty-three, his customary heater still bothered hitters; they were looking for it before the game even started. A veteran clubhouse attendant once said that before Ryan pitched, there were three times as many cups of coffee consumed by the opposing team than for any other pitcher in the game. The hitters might as well load up on caffeine, since hitting against seventy-five-mph pitches in batting practice is not much preparation for facing ninety-five-mph pitches in game situations.

Some hitters were so psyched out by Ryan that they didn't even bring their game bats up to the plate, fearing they'd wind up splintered in their hands. As Reggie Jackson described facing Ryan: "Every hitter likes fastballs, just like everybody likes ice cream. But you don't like it when someone's stuffing it into you by the gallon."

By and large, when someone like Ryan blows batters away, as he's done over 5,000 times, they don't really mind it. Hitters know they're in good company when they strike out. "It's quick and painless," explained Reggie Smith, who struck out twelve times against the Express.

At its peak, Ryan's fastball was so fast that the ball seemed to "explode" when it reached the plate, and that's not just sportswriters' jargon. Because the ball moves so fast, the human eye cannot adjust to it quickly enough. When the eye finally does adjust, as the ball reaches the plate, it suddenly appears normal-sized with what seems like an explosion of a million blinding specks.

The best fastball pitchers are often described as having a "hopping" fastball. But research has shown that there is no such thing as a rising fastball, even if it looks like it's literally jumping over the bat. The ball, being thrown faster than normal, just gives in to gravity less in coming down from over the pitcher's head on an elevated mound. The faster pitch just doesn't drop as much, and so the hitter swings under it. In *The Physics of Baseball,* Yale professor Robert Adair figured that for every 1.5 mph over ninety mph, the ball is about a foot quicker to the plate, and drops less, by about one inch. So the same swing that would connect solidly on the ninety-mph fastball will totally miss the ninety-six-mph fastball by four full inches.

Most major league hitters will tell you that the pitch that gives them the most trouble is an overpowering fastball with good movement on it. Even so, the good fastball hitters—and most major league hitters fit that description—remain confident that if they see enough of them, they'll eventually connect on anybody's heater. Even the peerless Ryan, after all, is only a little better than a .500 pitcher for his career. The power pitcher may strike out everybody in the first inning, but the fastball hitter will wait for him to lose a little something, keep him clocked, and then later in the game—pow!

Hitters, being vain and macho creatures, don't like to admit that they can't hit any pitcher's fastball, especially when it's up around the letters. Most hitters made it to the majors by killing the high fastball, so they don't easily admit that they can't get around on Vida Blue's or Dwight Gooden's or Roger Clemens's high hard one. The more the smart hitters face this type of pitcher, the more they learn about him, and they make adjustments. Pitchers with great fastballs often breeze through the league for their first year or even two. Then the hitters will try to lay off the pitch high in the strike zone that they literally can't hit, or stop trying to hit home runs, and just aim to make good contact.

Just as the hitter won't admit that he can't hit a pitcher's fastball, the pitcher falls in love with his fastball and believes nobody can hit it. Dwight Gooden admits his infatuation with throwing serious smoke, sometimes known as "gas," "dead red," or just "Number One." "There's no other feeling like it," said Gooden. "Throw your first fastball by a hitter and you never want to stop."

But Gooden knows that the fastball by itself, even the one-hundred-mph variety, is not enough. "I don't know what the speed is that a hitter absolutely couldn't catch up with," he said, "but I'll tell you what—no man has reached it yet." Bob Gibson had a nasty fastball, but he also acknowledged that it was still a mortal pitch. If the batter missed his fastball by a foot, he would throw another one, but if he just fouled it off, then he would think about throwing something else.

I remember an extra-inning game between the Tigers and the Red Sox in 1978, when John Hiller was a relief ace and Jim Rice at his best as a batter. Hiller threw Rice sixteen high fastballs in succession, and after a dozen Rice was just missing them as he fouled them right back to the screen. I turned to my friend in the stands and said, "This is the last pitch of the ballgame." Hiller threw another fastball and Rice crushed it, the ball clearing the high wall in deep left center by a foot. Challenging the Jim Rice of that season with one fastball after another was like challenging God, and God is statistically very tough in those situations.

The other fantasy of the die-hard fan who imagines himself a big-league hitter is the chance to cream one of those soft, room-service, off-speed pitches. I remember watching the supreme knuckleball artist Hoyt Wilhelm warm up at Tiger Stadium in the bullpen down the right-field line, anxious to see the break of the best knuckler in the business. It just looked like an easy toss, and I supposed you really had to be standing at the plate trying to hit it to get a sense of the ball movement. Then Wilhelm made a little wave, and his bullpen catcher put on the mask, and took a deep breath. The catcher didn't catch any of the next dozen pitches, even with the special oversized pancake glove, although he managed to knock some down. The deliveries fluttered and sailed, hung, dropped and rose, and hit him all over his body, as if Wilhelm had the ball on some invisible string.

A Wilhelm goes, a Gibson or Koufax retires, but life never gets easier for the hitters. The frequent use of relief pitchers means that hitters hardly ever face a really tired pitcher; often it's a fresh arm with a trick pitch. Also, the infields are perfectly groomed and on artificial turf hitters don't get the benefit of bad hops. The fielders' gloves are obscenely huge, so they catch everything unless it's really hit where they ain't. And pitchers don't give in to hitters as frequently as they used to.

"I think it's tougher to hit today, average-wise," Whitey Herzog told Tom Boswell. "When you get into pro ball, rookie league, you may never see a fastball on three and two. They might throw you a change or a curveball. You never used to see that, even when I was in the big leagues. The big thing in the old days, two-and-oh you'd see a lot of fastballs. You didn't see a lot of straight changes and stuff."

It just isn't a hitter's world anymore. Pitchers have the edge, and it's getting worse. Pitchers and pitching coaches are never satisfied with dominating hitters; they're always trying to invent new pitches, and some of them turn out to be very hard to hit. One important change was the invention of the slider, which came on the scene in the late 1940s. "The slider," said Ted Williams, "is probably as good a pitch as there is in baseball. All hitters have trouble with the slider; Mays says it's the toughest, Aaron says it's the toughest. I say it's the greatest pitch in baseball. It's easy to learn. It's easy to control. Immediately, it gives a pitcher a third or fourth pitch for his repertoire."

The important thing about the slider is that it gets the hitter off balance whether he's looking for a fastball or a curveball. It interferes with his timing. "When the slider came along," said former Red Sox slugger Walt Dropo, "it took a guy away from his sweet spot. And that's the whole purpose of a slider. . . . So the batter might miss a curveball, but hey, he'll maybe hit the slider, but he won't hit it hard, and he'll hit it on the ground. Bob Lemon threw sinkers in on you and sliders on the defensive. So he had you going both ways. You were always on the defensive. And that's a very difficult type of pitcher to hit."

Then there are the trick pitches, which dance or disappear down an invisible chute. The knuckleball, however, is something of a dinosaur in today's game. It still has its working practitioners, like Tom Candiotti of the Indians and Charlie Hough of the Rangers, but few have been able to master it in the manner of Wilhelm or Phil Niekro. Today the most common "slip pitch," which appears to be a strike before diving down into the dirt, is the split-finger fastball.

The splitter is a descendant of the off-speed forkball thrown by reliever Elroy Face of the Pirates, who compiled an incredible 18–1 record out of the bullpen in 1959. Roger Craig was then pitching for the Dodgers, and he was suitably impressed; he soon began experimenting. The forkball is thrown with the forefinger and middle finger spread wide, and released with a strong snap of the wrist. Craig's contribution, after years of tinkering, was to develop the forker as a split-finger fastball by not wedging the ball so deeply in the palm of the hand.

His most famous and accomplished disciple was Mike Scott, a floundering, desperate pitcher who was traded from the Mets to the Astros after the 1982 season. Scott then spent a week with Craig, mastered the pitch quickly with his huge right hand, and within a few years was the dominant pitcher in the National League.

After adopting the splitter, Scott won the 1986 Cy Young award, throwing a no-hitter in the division clincher, and he became the oldest man ever to strike out over 300 batters in a season. Umpire Doug Harvey marveled at the split-finger: "It's a fastball that just explodes like a bomb!"

With all these advances, and computerized charts kept on what pitches you can hit and what you can't, it's no wonder that at some point every hitter must confront that dreaded malady—the batting slump. All it takes is a few line drives that are caught, a few sure homers that curve just foul, a few bad calls by the umpire, and, before you know it, the hitter's in a "slump." Joe Morgan once went zero for thirty-five late in his career with the Phillies, but he said: "I'm not in a slump. I'm just not getting any hits." Morgan wasn't evading reality. He knew he was seeing the ball well and hitting it hard, so there was no need to worry. Hitters try to tell themselves that the breaks of the game will even out, but they have to believe that, or else their batting struggles would certainly drive them batty.

The batting slump was born with the birth of baseball, perhaps accelerated today by the high technology of pitching. But every hitter in history had slumps, no matter how skilled. A hitter goes through weeks where he misses pitches he usually nails, and starts chasing pitches he usually takes. The slightest hesitation creeps into a batter's approach, and he's dead. Bobby Murcer described a typical at-bat during a slump: "You decide you'll wait for your pitch. Then, as the ball starts toward the plate, you think about your stance; and then you think about your swing; and then you realize the ball that went past you for a strike was your pitch."

Bill Doran's 1989 slump lasted half a season, but he kept his sense of humor, saying that he wasn't even going to call it a slump anymore, but "a doran." Andy Van Slyke had a miserable, injury-riddled year as well, and finally admitted that he had tried everything—hitting to the opposite field, hitting up the middle, pulling the ball, hitting the ball on the ground and in the air. He even tried *not* hitting the ball, but that didn't work, either. Van Slyke's approach to a slump, like Doran's, is to find the perfect self-deprecating line that will enable him to laugh at the game that's laughing at him. In his ability to joke about any atrocity he committed out on the field, Andy Van was closing in on the all-time leaders—Bill Lee, Mickey Rivers, and Yogi Berra. When he hit a glitch early in 1990, Andy got off this beauty: "Right now I couldn't drive home Miss Daisy."

Of course, the hitters most prone to slumps are the inexperienced. "Hitting is confidence," Bill Buckner told Roger Angell. "It's the feeling that you can hit certain pitchers in certain situations. The hard things for young hitters is knowing that—just knowing they can do the job." Even talented rookies generally have to go through this rite of passage. Mike Schmidt hit .196 as a rookie, and Robin Ventura of the White Sox underwent the same trial by fire in his 1990 rookie season. He had been a three-time All-American at Oklahoma State and set an NCAA record with a fifty-eight-game hitting streak. In the big leagues he went zero for forty-one.

"People suggested that I rub my batting helmet or shave my head," Ventura said. He didn't offer burning incense, rum, and Colonel Sanders' fried chicken to Jo-Bu, the bat god, as fictional slugger Pedro Cerrano did in the movie *Major League,* but he did change his number from twenty-one to twenty-three, which was worn by another notable athlete in Chicago, Michael Jordan. His teammates tried rally caps, visor tweaks, the laying on of hands, and then wore headbands reading "Get a Knock," after which Ventura finally got four hits in his next two games. Despite all the voodoolike hoopla, Ventura credited breaking out of it to staying with what he always did.

Making adjustments can plunge the hitter into a frighteningly complex maze, as Reggie Jackson described it to Angell. "You begin to understand how many little things there are that might be wrong with what you're doing. If you know you're dragging the bat through the hitting zone, say, it might be because you're lowering your hands, which causes them not to be back in the right hitting position, or you might be wrapping the bat around your neck, which causes the swing to get a little longer, or you could be dropping the head of the bat, which causes you to top the ball, or you could be pulling off the ball, which causes your front shoulder to fly out. Those are just a few of the possibilities. Anything that changes your regular swing is going to mess up your natural feeling at the plate, and if you're not natural you're nothing: you're in a slump."

But hitters can help themselves to come out of a slump. Paul Blair's solution was to bunt for a hit as soon as he went zero for eight, "anything to get that shit off me." Generally a hitter beats a slump by hitting the ball back through the middle of the diamond, and eventually gets his timing and confidence back. Ty Cobb maintained that every hitter has to have a plan to get out of a slump. His was to move up close, right on top of the plate. "You see," he said, "when I went into a slump, it was because I was chasing pitches out of the strike zone. By moving up in the box and getting closer to the plate, I eliminated my margin of error in judging which pitches were strikes. I knew that if I didn't have to back off, the pitch was over the plate. And if the pitch was away at all, it was a ball."

All the great hitters come back to the importance of seeing the ball. As Ted Williams said, "I had a lot of big days, because I was always the same. I had the same attitude whether I was oh for three or three for three. I know that when you're concentrating on getting a hit, you won't see the ball as well. But when you're concentrating on seeing the ball, you'll hit it well, and then the hits will take care of themselves."

As the hits begin to fall in, the ball that looked like an aspirin during the slump starts looking like a baseball again, or even a grapefruit. Quickly, the pendulum can swing back to that hitter's state of grace called "seeing it good." Then a hitter can go on a real streak. Nobody was ever hotter than Walt Dropo in 1952 when he had twelve consecutive base hits over three games. "You don't know why it happens to you," he said. "You get in that groove. I don't care what they threw at me, I always seemed to get good wood on it—line drives. I didn't hit any home runs out of the twelve, so that means I was swinging parallel—making good contact. I didn't change anything."

For Tommy Davis, the ex-Dodger star, relaxation was the key. "But I don't know if that can be taught. I just don't know. They used to call me lazy or lackadaisical, but the lazier I felt the better I'd hit."

When a hitter is relaxed and confident, he can get "locked in," as they sometimes call it, entering that "sweet spot in time," a confluence of strength, timing, and technique. Glenn Davis, now with Baltimore, tried to explain this feeling, and why he usually hits his homers in bunches. "It's muscle memory taking over," he said.

In 1990 Andre Dawson got into the perfect hitter's groove early in the season. His bat was so quick that he could be looking for a change-up and still hit the fastball out of the park. As pitcher Jay Howell put it, "It's pretty obvious the ball looks like a basketball to him now. He can hit the high pitch out of the strike zone, has a real nice level swing on the ball that's up, so you can't necessarily say you will pitch him up and in, low and away. He has such long arms, and when he's leaning out over the plate, he can hit the low-and-away pitch. When he's hot like he is now, there isn't a zone you can play with. It all just becomes a big mistake zone."

Now for the heartbreaking part of being a hot hitter. Not only doesn't the streak last, but it can be the cause of another nosedive, because a hitting spree can change a batter's outlook and mental approach to hitting just as drastically as a slump can. All of a sudden a guy is red hot, and he starts trying to figure out what he's doing to hit the ball so well, or he tries to repeat an earlier perfect swing, or he starts thinking about his soaring statistics—and then he's off his game again. After a stretch of hitting over .400, a hitter naturally starts to wonder, especially if he doesn't do it very often, if he really is that good. If his psyche can't support that new level he's on, doubt will naturally creep in, and before he knows it, he's zero for twelve.

The tragic fact of life for the hitter is that real mastery over major league pitchers is impossible. After all, hitting is based on failure. Even the all-time greats never succeed in hitting safely as much as 40 percent of the time over a career. The benchmark of the good hitter is three hits out of ten tries. The difference between a .250 hitter and a .300 hitter is only twenty-five hits over 500 at-bats, or about a hit per week over a six-month season. It takes a whole season sometimes for the cream to rise to the top, and this is what the batting average indicates, this consistency over the long haul.

A lot of players say they don't follow their averages in the papers. That's not because they don't care, but because it's too important— it's their livelihood. The most embarrassing thing is when they're hitting under .200, and it's flashed up on one of those giant scoreboards under their picture when they come up to the plate. They can only hope the fans think it's a clerical error.

But hitters have always known that the batting average, as a statistic, is vastly overrated. How silly was it that Roger Maris was not only criticized but nearly drawn and quartered for having the nerve to break Babe Ruth's home-run record in 1961 while hitting a measly .269? What counted then as now was getting on base, scoring, and driving in runs; as long as Maris walked ninety-four times, scored 132 runs, and drove in 142, it didn't matter much that he didn't get the dozen extra singles that would have made him a .290 hitter.

Today, broadcasters and fans, coaches and managers—everyone in baseball really—pays a lot more attention to On Base Average and Hitting with Runners in Scoring Position, stats that are masked by the batting average. The statistical game has become much more complex. Fans now want to know what players hit against lefties and righties, and in late-inning pressure situations when they were in the midst of a hangover. It seems sometimes that there are more factfinders than facts, but the host of new numbers available—the computer age has had its impact in baseball—has undoubtedly led to greater understanding in deciphering what the numbers mean.

At the same time the longer a statistical record lasts, the more meaning it has. Almost everyone agrees that the hardest record to break will be Joe DiMaggio's fifty-six-game hitting streak, part of the reason being the blizzard of media attention that a long hitting streak attracts. In DiMaggio's time no one paid much attention to the streak until it hit twenty-five. Today everyone knows when a batter has a *six*-game streak going. But if the DiMaggio record is sacrosanct, other imposing batting marks have been surpassed. Ruth and Cobb, maybe, each in his own way, the greatest hitters of all time, have had their most renowned and long-standing career marks taken away from them. When Aaron hit homer number 715 and Rose punched his hit number 4,192 to left field, two career records fell that had once seemed unbreakable. (Cobb, however, still holds the highest lifetime average, .367.) When Roger Maris broke the Babe's record of sixty home runs, Ruth's record was thirty-four years old; Maris's record is already thirty years old. Even though Maris and Aaron stripped from him his season and then career homer records, Ruth still has a

host of imposing, lesser-known marks that few have approached—
the record for single-season slugging percentage, total bases, number
of walks, and home runs per at-bat.

The oddities and coincidences of baseball's numbers game are
enough to give the most hard-line empiricist pause in the wee hours.
What are the odds, after all, that the player who is ranked number
one on the all-time home-run list would also be listed first alphabet-
ically in the players' register? You can look him up: Henry Aaron is
right before his brother Tommie.

Arts of Deception

There is a basic primal element in the confrontation of the pitcher and the hitter that connects us with our earliest past. Pick up a stone, you want to throw it; pick up a stick, you want to hit something, or somebody, with it. Baseball pairs these two basic Neanderthal activities—the pitcher's windup and throw, and the batter's uncoiling swing—and presents them in a scientific showcase of point and counterpoint developed over the last hundred years.

The war between pitchers and hitters has evolved into a monumentally complex game of cat and mouse, where the pitcher changes the location, break, and speed of his pitches in a sequence meant to confound the hitter. "Hitting is timing," said Warren Spahn in his near-perfect summation, "and pitching is upsetting timing."

Sandy Koufax, one of the most dominant pitchers of the postwar period, didn't have to fool hitters. Almost disdainfully, he gave away what he would throw. In the stretch position, for instance, he held his elbows out before delivering his curve. But that just tipped off the batter as to what pitch he was going to strike out on. Nobody had that much success against Koufax (except, oddly, career .200 hitter Bob Uecker).

The vast majority of pitchers, however, don't even dream of having Koufax's stuff, and that's where guile, craft, and experience come in. Most pitchers who stick around in the big leagues for more than a few years make their living by fooling hitters. Deception starts before the ball ever leaves the pitcher's hand. In his windup, the pitcher tries to hide the ball before the release, and may also try to distract the hitter at the same time. Fernando Valenzuela used a high leg kick and stared up at passing planes with his eyes rolled back in his head, which can bother hitters who want the pitcher to know where they're standing. Stu Miller, the Oriole reliever from the early '60s, became an All-Star with a collection of junk pitches. He owed his success to jerking his neck just before he threw, which upset the timing of hitters.

The good hitter will ignore these movements, or any others, such as flailing limbs, flopping greasy hair, a tongue hanging out, or even the pitcher suddenly going cross-eyed. "I don't look at the pitcher," said Keith Hernandez in his heyday. "I look at the zone above his shoulder where he'll release the ball." Some hitters do just try to pick up the ball and swing, but most of the good ones train their eyes to pick up what pitch it is by the rotation of the ball, its various spins, almost as soon as it leaves the pitcher's hand, as Hernandez certainly did. If the pitch is a slider, for instance, it can be identified by a red dot on the ball, formed by the crossways spinning of the seams.

A slow, herky-jerky windup like the one used by the Mets' Sid Fernandez frequently confuses hitters, who all complain about his late release. Sid the Squid short-arms the ball so it comes right out of his white uniform shirt, making it hard to pick up the ball. Pitching coach Tom House made a study of the pitchers who were considered "sneaky-fast"—guys whose fastballs did not register in the nineties on the radar guns, but whose pitches were on top of hitters before they could get ready. He found that they gained extra "speed" by keeping hitters from recognizing their release points, often by throwing up their front elbows as they came forward.

Of the various ways of tricking, fooling, deceiving, or misleading the hitter, the primary element in all of it comes down to pitch selection, or, What do I throw now and where do I throw it? There are indeed dozens of variables that may determine what the pitcher might throw on a given pitch: what pitches are working for him in that game, his history with that batter, how that batter's been doing of late against the whole league, how the wind is blowing (curveballs break more when thrown into the wind; but high fastballs thrown into the wind will be a tad slower, and go out of the park faster and easier), the dimensions of the ballpark (if it's short down the line, you might not give the batter anything to pull in a close game), and the umpire's working strike zone for this particular game, not to mention the score, the game situation, and the time of day. When the shadows fall between the mound and the batter in late afternoon, it's tough to hit anything, and when twilight settles over the park, even if the lights are turned on, the fastball is even harder to see.

This is just a small sample of a nearly endless feed of information, but a pitcher processes most of it instinctively. Once a pitcher feels confident of three or even four pitches, he can get into the flow of the game, and the decision of what to throw becomes more automatic. "Then," said Mike Flanagan, "it's like a game of pool when you plan three or four moves ahead. One thing sets up another."

Sometimes a pitcher will decide what pitch to throw by looking at the batter. Reggie Jackson said a hitter should always walk up there with a swagger, as if he owned the pitcher, even if you're zero for fourteen against him. "He might forget," said Reggie. On the other hand, a hitter's body language can tip off the pitcher, especially once the batter takes his stance at the plate. How he holds the bat is one of the hitter's signatures that a pitcher can instantly read from the mound.

"I could tell a hitter's weaknesses," said Gaylord Perry, "the first time I ever saw him, just by watching him take his stance. Like, if a hitter carries the bat high and wraps it back around his neck, well, then you know he can't hit the fastball in on his hands. It takes him too long to get the bat started and clear his hips out of the way.

"And if the hitter holds the bat low or lays it out away from him, then he can't hit the outside pitch with authority, especially the breaking ball. You can get him to pull the trigger too soon.

"Also, you gotta watch their feet. The good hitters, like Rod Carew or Eddie Murray, they had a half-dozen different stances and they'd change 'em between pitches. That's how you tell what they're guessing." Pitchers especially don't like it if a hitter changes his stance in the middle of a windup. When that happened, Perry felt that the pitcher's job was to drill the batter with the fastball.

When Keith Hernandez was a Cardinal, Lou Brock suggested that he move closer to the plate, thus acquiring the outside corner as his territory. "They'll try and beat you inside," Brock warned. "Look for the inside pitch." Hernandez looked inside, pitchers threw inside, and he hit it.

Sometimes a batter won't give away what he's looking for until the pitch is thrown, which is why some pitchers think it's a good idea, if it's a key situation, to throw the first pitch out of the strike zone. If the batter is hungry for a pitch out over the plate, he'll lean in; if he's looking to pull an inside pitch, he'll open his stance when he strides as the pitch is thrown.

Even as the pitcher is trying to read what the hitter is doing, he can get "deked" himself. Hitters will sometimes try to fool the pitcher by moving up in the batter's box, as if to hit a curveball before its sharp break, when the hitter is really trying to set the pitcher up to throw a fastball. Some hitters might even take a bad swing at a pitch, hoping the pitcher will throw it again sometime later in the game.

Darrell Evans remembered how his teammate on the Atlanta Braves, Hank Aaron, used to employ this stratagem. "Every time he faced a new pitcher, Hank wanted to hit him that first time up at bat, so he would own him forever. He would walk up there, and if he knew the guy had a good breaking ball, he would swing at one in the dirt and miss it on purpose. Now he knows they're going to throw him another one. And the next curve that they hung, he hit it out, and they never knew what he was doing."

Great pitchers practice the same kind of deception. Whitey Ford, a past master of the games within the game, would throw a so-so curveball early in the count, and then later strike the guy out with his sharp-breaking curve. Walt Dropo remembered what it was like facing Ford. "He'd start you out one way one time, and he'd start you out another way another time. The first time he might start you out with a curveball outside. Next time he might start you with a curveball inside. He's setting you up and you're looking inside, outside, and you're hesitating. He might give you the fastball, but you hesitated that fraction of a second, and he's got you. It was like a chess game with him. You couldn't get that bat on the ball. He took the bat right out of your hands."

The old reliable way of working a hitter is with fastballs inside and change-ups away, guaranteed to keep the hitter off balance. Bob Ojeda invariably set up hitters this way, popping the fastball on their fists, and then throwing his "dead fish" change over the outside corner, getting the right-handed batter to swing way too early. Why don't hitters wise up to this kind of thing, when it's so obvious what Ojeda's trying to do? Ask Von Hayes, who faced Ojeda and looked, unbelieving, at three consecutive fastballs pretty much right down the middle. The change in the pattern just blew the hitter's mind; Hayes couldn't believe that Ojeda would ever pitch him that way, and that's why sometimes the best pitch is the most obvious pitch.

Often it's not important to fool the hitter totally. Some pitchers like to give the hitter just what he wants—almost. Let's say a hitter is a known first-ball high fastball hitter. The pitcher throws him the high fastball, but just a little higher than he likes it, up where he can't really hit it. That's how Dennis Eckersley coined his term for the fastball—"the cheese"—as bait for the hitter.

Of course, a pitcher cannot play with a hitter in this fashion unless he has control. Tim Belcher of the Dodgers once walked 133 batters in 163 innings in the minors. Then he finally found out where the plate was, and realized, after a successful game against the Padres, "Pitching is a lot like real estate: location, location, location."

While the hitters generally stay pretty much the same, the pitchers must constantly adjust to keep one step ahead. That means, in the context of a single game, that the pitcher must not show his full array of pitches, so he can vary the pattern the second time through, and then mix it up again if he gets to the third time. "The toughest pitchers," said Darrell Evans, "were the ones who would never throw you the same pitch twice in a row in the same location. And they would try not to show you how they were going to try and get you out the third or fourth time up when the game was on the line."

But pitchers must do more than give hitters a new look as they face them in a particular game. Invariably a pitcher will have to overhaul his arsenal and throw different pitches at different points in his career. As the blazing heater slows down, many a fastball pitcher comes to rely on sliders and sinkers as out pitches to prolong his career.

Lefty Grove, one of the most dominating pitchers in baseball history, realized that even he had to make adjustments to keep winning. Listen to the late cerebral catcher, Moe Berg: "Grove was a fastball pitcher and the hitters knew it. The hitters looked for this pitch; Lefty did not try to fool them by throwing anything else. . . . In 1935 Lefty had recovered from his first serious sore arm and the grind of many seasons had taken their toll. Now he had changed his tactics, and was pitching curves and fastballs, one or the other. His control was practically perfect. On a day in that year in Washington, Heinie Manush, a great hitter, was at bat with two men on the bases. The game was at stake, the count was three balls and two strikes. Heinie stood there, confident, looking for Lefty's fastball. 'Well,' thought Heinie, 'it might be a curve.' Lefty was throwing the curve more and more now, but the chances with the count of three and two were that Lefty would throw his fastball with everything he had. Fast or curve—he couldn't throw anything else; he had nothing else to throw. Heinie broke his back striking out on the next pitch, the first forkball Grove ever threw. For over a year, on the sidelines, in the bullpen, between pitching starts, Lefty had practically perfected this pitch before he threw it, and he waited for a crucial spot to use it." Grove kept going into the 1941 season, retiring that year after winning his three-hundredth game. Guile helped carry him into the Hall of Fame.

The pitcher generally does not plot these grand new battle plans by himself. The pitching coach is usually involved, and during games the pitcher often allows the catcher to call most of the game. In some cases, after working together for years, pitcher and catcher establish a special unspoken rapport. Even though Steve Carlton pitched with cotton stuffed in his ears and didn't need to hear anything his catcher had to say, he nonetheless had a special relationship with his battery mate, Tim McCarver. Carlton grew to not even think of the hitter; he was just playing, in his mind, "an elevated game of catch."

McCarver tried to make it difficult for hitters to figure out the pitching pattern he was using, so sometimes he would call for an out-of-character pitch, simply to hide the real pattern until a key situation arose and he really had to get the hitter out. "If you throw the curve on three-two for a strike in the first inning," McCarver explained, "when it'd be easier just to go with the fastball and stay away from the aggravation of a walk, you might put an oh for four on the guy.

All day he's going to think you have complete confidence in your curveball, even if you really don't."

Some hitters do try to get into the catchers' heads, spot *their* patterns. Will a catcher call for pitches that he can't hit? Or will he tend to call for a pitch that the batter swung and missed on? Vain about a baserunner stealing, does he call for the fastball, especially if he thinks he has a chance of throwing the runner out?

Catchers want the batter to think about what they're doing to him, which is why some catchers have a signal for the pitcher to just pretend to be shaking off the sign. If the pitcher takes too much time looking in at his catcher, then hitters don't like it, and instead of tensing up or relaxing too much at the plate, they will call for time and step out of the box.

Some pitchers tend to get upset when a hitter takes too much time adjusting his batting glove, pants, helmet, and cup. Mike Hargrove was the all-time champ when it came to fussing around the batter's box, earning the title of "The Human Rain Delay." Dave Magadan of the Mets requires a stopwatch to get him in the batter's box. He takes a lot of pitches and fouls off nearly as many, ensuring the maximum amount of time on television. But Magadan also winds up swinging at very few bad pitches, and hardly ever strikes out.

The batter is trying to find that perfect balance between intensity and relaxation, between thinking of the situation and letting his instincts loose. One classic respite from the batter-pitcher wars occurred late in the 1961 season in Detroit when Roger Maris was chasing Ruth's record. Maris had become so pressured by the effort to hit sixty homers in 154 games that he developed a nervous skin condition and was informed by his barber that his hair was falling out in tufts. Nearly in tears, Maris told manager Ralph Houk that he couldn't play. He was persuaded to start the game, and came up in the late innings against Tiger reliever Terry Fox.

He had hit fifty-seven homers up to that point. As he dug his spikes in, he felt wracked by tension, and stepped out of the box. Just as he looked up, a flock of geese came over the right field roof in formation. He watched them flying for a full minute. Then he wiped his brow, stepped back in to hit, and drove Fox's first pitch into the stands in right for number fifty-eight. Years later he told Tony Kubek that he could still see those geese, they were just so peaceful to watch.

If Ted Williams was hitting in a tight spot and a big black cloud suddenly covered the sun, he would yell "Time!," step out of the box, put his finger in his eye, and complain about a cinder. "Unless you know for a fact that your eyes can dilate quickly enough in that split second to adjust to a light that might be half the candle power, you'd be foolish to stand in there and try to hit. Step out and wait until the cloud passes, or until your eyes have dilated and are accustomed to the new light."

Rusty Staub used to step out of the box at Shea Stadium in New York when a plane was passing noisily overhead so it wouldn't interfere with his concentration. He stopped that practice when he discovered that the noise would make it difficult for the fielders to gauge how solidly he had hit the ball, and make it hard for them to get a good jump. And so Le Grand Orange adapted, and learned to hit with the drone of jets buzzing in his ears.

In short, pitchers and hitters will do anything to get an edge on each other. Sometimes the performers bend the rules. Pitchers, for instance, have been known to doctor the ball. It was legal early in the century, when the two pitchers who won forty games in a season, Jack Chesbro and Ed Walsh, each threw The Spitter. The spitball was banned in 1920, but for an interim period the established pitchers who threw the wet one were allowed to keep throwing it. Burleigh Grimes, who retired in 1934, was the last of the pitchers to use the spitter legally. From then on, all pitchers had to hide their loading of the ball, producing an awesome lore of stories and controversies.

Once his career was over, Brooklyn Dodgers pitcher Preacher Roe told all in a *Sports Illustrated* article in 1955. He was a mediocre pitcher until he adopted the illegal pitch in 1948, and had a ninety-three–thirty-seven record over the rest of his career. Roe used to ingeniously spit on his glove just after delivering the ball, so nobody would see him loading up his fingers because they were watching the pitch. He also used to spit on the meat of his hand as he pretended to wipe off his brow with his elbow.

But Roe only said he threw it a couple of times in a game. In 1971 Whitey Ford poured out his totally unrepentant cheatin' heart in an article for *The New York Times* entitled "Confessions of a Gunkball Artist." Ford admitted that the "Chairman of the Board" owed his career accomplishments to his total disregard for the rules. His gunkball was a pitch loaded with a homemade concoction of turpentine, baby oil, and resin, and old Whitey regularly took the mound with this gunk all over his hands, uniform, and cap.

Ford doctored the ball in every way he could find, even if it meant getting down and dirty. He would spit all around the mound making little mudpies, then bend down to tie his shoe and load up the ball. In one 1963 World Series game against the Dodgers, Ford said, "I used enough mud that day to build a dam."

He was also a scuffball artiste who went out to the mound wearing a ring on his glove hand that had a rasp on it, covered by a flesh-colored Band-Aid. Ford could scuff the ball anytime he rubbed it up in his hands. "It was as though I had my own tool bench out there."

Gaylord Perry was the only one with the baseball chutzpah to publish his confessions in a book (*Me and the Spitter*) *while* he was still playing. He had begun throwing the wet one, like so many other spitballers, when his career was foundering, and he had astonishing success with it. When Perry first began with the spitball, he was "a slobberer," meaning that you could see the spit flying off the ball in flight, and it would even make a splashing sound in the catcher's mitt. The Giants' infielders had to become adept at throwing the spitter themselves because when they fielded a grounder, it would invariably be wet. Bobby Bonds claimed he dropped a fly ball in the outfield because it was so loaded with Perry's saliva.

Eventually Perry grew to have disdain for other slobberers and their vulgar spitball etiquette, as he became a true master of the pitch, finding that a reduced load of saliva actually gave him better control. One of his first tricks was to wet the back of his thumb while wetting his first two fingers. Then he would wipe off the fingers, and flick them over his thumb to wet them again.

After the rule was made forbidding pitchers from going to their mouths, Perry experimented with every substance in the slippery world of lubricants. "I reckon I tried everything on the old apple but salt and pepper and chocolate sauce toppin'." On the recommendation of his family doctor, he began using K-Y jelly. It worked well, but it was not as long-lasting as Perry would have liked. "If I had a long inning," he said, "my K-Y reserves would run pretty low. I had to give up vaginal jelly."

The all-around best ball lubricant he ever found was Vaseline. He would take the mound with a thin smear on his face and neck that blended in with his sweat and was even slicker than spit. "The Good Lord," he said, "blessed me with oily skin." He could just touch his forehead and be able to throw two greaseballs, or he could touch his wrist, ear, pants, cap, shirt, shoes, or belt. Perry smelled like a pharmacy, and that's why Billy Martin once brought a bloodhound trained to sniff Vaseline to the ballpark.

The number of pitchers who have been punished for these tactics is a select group. The umpires just haven't had the backing of their league offices to punish cheaters, as was evident in the case of Don Sutton, so widely suspected of scuffing the ball that he became known as "Black & Decker." (The San Francisco Giants, with pitcher Bud Black and rookie catcher Steve Decker, actually have such a battery.)

Sutton never admitted that he did anything illegal on the mound, even when the dean of National League umps, Doug Harvey, ejected him from a game for scuffing balls. Sutton threatened to sue Harvey if he was suspended, on the grounds that it would be depriving him of earning a living. The league backed off and said Sutton wasn't ejected for doctoring the ball, but was ejected for *throwing* balls that happened to be scuffed. Policing scuffballs, like policing the spitter, became something of a joke. When other umpires searched Sutton, an umpire found a note in his glove that read, "You're getting warm, but it's not here!"

There were pitchers who really lived off of deception. For instance, Lew Burdette of the Milwaukee Braves was a spitball master. Former player and manager Pat Corrales said he saw Burdette beat the Cubs one time on 105 pitches. "Ninety-eight were wet, and that's the gospel truth," he said. Burdette used to make an elaborate display of spitting on his fingers, and then make equally elaborate fake wipe-offs. More than any pitcher, Burdette liked to use the spitter as a psychological weapon, as a head game he played with the hitters. "My best pitch," he used to say coyly, and even with the occasional wink, "is the one I don't throw."

If the hitter thinks that the pitcher might throw a spitball, that's just another pitch he has to consider, another advantage for the pitcher in the mental game of outguessing each other. For all the opinions Ted Williams had about the swing itself, he was also a big proponent of getting a good ball to hit; and that meant having a good idea of what the pitcher was going to throw, and being ready for it. Stan Musial was known as the kind of hitter who could hit the pitcher's pitch, but Williams was the one who made an art out of getting the good pitch to hit in the right zone.

Williams developed an elephant's memory for everything a pitcher had thrown him, in previous games as well as the matchup at hand. If he looked bad on a pitch, he would look for the same pitch again, maybe later in the game, and then cream it. In the wake of the havoc that Williams wreaked on the American League, more and more hitters started keeping a "book" on opposing pitchers, either writing down or keeping in their heads what was thrown to them in what sequence, and in what game situations.

But keeping a book in today's game could better be described as keeping a television show, because many of the top hitters, such as Tony Gwynn and Will Clark, have their teams record video libraries of all their at-bats, and have them filed by specific pitchers in the league. So before they face a particular pitcher, they might watch all the at-bats they had against him the previous year, or earlier in the season, to review the patterns that he uses. Will Clark will not watch himself in these videos, boasting that his swing "stays pretty much the same." He chooses to watch the pitchers—every move they make, every breath they take—when he's up at bat.

Besides studying pitchers, there was another secret to Williams's success in getting a good ball to hit. He was such a naturally gifted fastball hitter that he could look for breaking pitches and still hit the fastball when he got it. Hardly any other hitter could do that.

After Hank Aaron retired, Davey Johnson asked Aaron what he looked for at bat—if there was any pattern to his thinking. He told Johnson, "I looked for the same pitch my whole career. A breaking ball. All the time. I never worried about the fastball. They couldn't throw it past me. None of 'em."

Darrell Evans told me, "When you're swinging the bat good, and you're quick, you can put one pitch out of your mind, the fastball, because you know you can hit it all the time. You don't worry about the fastball because, if anything, you have a tendency to be too quick when you're feeling strong."

Howard Johnson adopted this philosophy in 1989 with the Mets when he started looking for the curve and set himself to just react to the fastball if he got it. In the off-season, Johnson had worked on speeding up his hand-eye coordination without a bat in his hands by pressing assorted buttons on a machine, reacting to different flashing lights. Confident that he could always hit the fastball, he was able to "guess curve" most of the time and ended up with the best year of his career.

All good hitters are guess hitters when they get ahead in the count 3–0, 3–1, or 2–0; they then become dangerous "zone hitters," looking for a particular pitch in a particular location. But Lou Piniella maintained that against the handful of great pitchers, the count advantage for the hitter wasn't much help. "Those are the guys who can either challenge you and get away with it—put it right in your zone and dare you to hit it—or the ones who consistently outguess you, who always have you lookin' at that three-one strike. But even with them, you've gotta make your own guess and get ready for a ball in your zone, because once or twice a game, even those guys are gonna lose their rhythm or try to do too much with a ball, and if you're not ready, that's a real lost opportunity. The only real difference between the good pitchers and the great ones is that the great ones don't yield to the situation around them. They're kind of self-contained, and they're gonna make you hit their pitch, not yours."

Tommy John had an interesting approach when the count was 2–0, making it work to his advantage. He would throw a pitch out of the strike zone. "They expect you to throw them a strike, so they swing at a pitch that they would normally take for a ball."

Keith Hernandez didn't wait to get up in the count; he zoned all the time against lefties. Against a left-handed pitcher, until he had two strikes on him, he would usually play a zone, looking either inside or out. With two strikes, everything changed, and he no longer cared to know the pitch or the zone. "If I knew the pitch I'd have a tendency to relax. Better for me is the split-second decision."

When the hitter has two strikes on him, he generally has to become more defensive, and just make contact on anything close. Jim Palmer felt that successful pitching could be boiled down to "staying ahead in the count and enlarging the strike zone."

Sometimes the best the hitter can do is foul off a series of unhittable "pitcher's pitches" until he can get one to drive. One of the most famous and dramatic home runs in World Series history was Bernie Carbo's three-run pinch-hit job in Game Six of the 1975 World Series, but he was able to tie the game with that hit only because of his ability to foul off a very tough pitch with two strikes on him. The fastball came in on him and he was jammed silly. Carbo swung feebly and late, and just managed to tick the ball off the handle of the bat. His next swing—bingo!

A few pitchers insist that the good hitters will hit the pitcher's pitch anyway, so the best thing to do is just lay in a batting practice fastball. "Why not?" said Jim Kern, former relief ace for the Indians and Rangers. "Let 'em get themselves out," he told me. "Let 'em kill the second baseman." Oil Can Boyd felt the same. "You get out bad hitters with good stuff, and you get out good hitters with bad stuff. You make a good pitch to a good hitter, *they like that.* That's what makes Wade Boggs such a good hitter, you pitch him inside and he can line that ball to left field."

The folklore of pitching abounds. If a pitcher travels around the minors and then maybe gets traded a few times in the majors, he hears them all. Throw the curve to guys under thirty. Throw the curve early in the year when the hitters are strong, and the fastball in the dog days of August when the hitters are tired. Often such tales have a racist tinge: Latin players are sometimes characterized as "first-ball high-ball hitters"; or you have to "jam the black guys." Gates Brown, former pinch-hitter extraordinaire and hitting instructor for the Tigers in 1984, put all of this unscientific balderdash in perspective when he declared, "If a man's wearing glasses, pitch him low and away."

Some pitchers think you can get too caught up in what you're going to throw. Like the hitter who is thinking up at the plate instead of just reacting to the ball, a pitcher may fall into the same trap. The pitch that a pitcher believes in will probably work better than the "right pitch" that he's not fully committed to throwing.

Before a big game between Baltimore and Oakland in the '70s, third baseman Sal Bando was pumping all-time saves leader Rollie Fingers for how he was going to pitch Frank Robinson and Brooks Robinson, so that Bando could position himself properly in the field.

Rollie said, "I'm going to pitch those suckers the best way I know how."

"But what are you going to throw to Frank?" Bando pleaded. "What are you going to throw to Brooks?"

Fingers stared off into the distance, and then turned to the A's captain. "Tell me again," Fingers replied. "Which one is which?"

PART 2

THE MANAGER'S

GAME

The Necessities

HELP WANTED: GRIZZLED VETERAN, EXPERIENCE PREFERRED, FOR LEADER-SHIP OF BASEBALL TEAM. ONLY THICK-SKINNED NEED APPLY. HIGH PAY, HIGH PRESSURE, HIGH TIMES. TRAVEL GALORE TO WELL-POPULATED AMERICAN CITIES, STAY IN BEST HOTELS. SUNFLOWER-SEED OR TOBACCO-CHEWER OKAY. NO HEAVY LIFTING.

A plum job, it sounds like, but wait. . . . Think of the number of things a manager is responsible for—the tactical moves, handling petulant players who make more money than he does, being constantly second-guessed and often lambasted by the press, roasted by unruly fans, and always put under pressure from the team's front office to *win*.

And yet, there's hardly a player who wouldn't like to manage in the majors. But few are called. If the odds of a player making it to the majors have been calculated as high as a million to one, the odds of becoming one of twenty-six big-league managers, the on-field brains of a multi-million-dollar sports franchise, are incalculable. And the odds broaden out even more when you note the revolving door in managers' alley—fired managers frequently in line to manage another team once *that* manager gets the sack. And on and on, ad infinitum. Becoming a big-league manager is a little like becoming President of the United States.

The jobs do have elements in common. As Commander-in-Chief, Ronald Reagan showed how to delegate authority so that he would not lose any valuable nap time, dozing through cabinet meetings. President Reagan even slept through the knocking down of a Libyan jet by American fighter planes, saying later that his aides would have woken him up if an American plane had gone down. All of this has rousing parallels to Casey Stengel in his later years: Casey sleeping on the Mets bench in the middle innings. Nobody said that made Casey unqualified to manage such a horrible team, but then again his napping was never a threat to national security.

Managers must delegate with the same impunity as Chief Executives. They have hitting coaches, pitching coaches, infielding coaches, and often a designated coach who brings the umpire the lineup card. There's a team captain to help the players organize their social activities on off-days, and of course a trainer to help the players deal with pulled muscles and hangovers. Billy Martin even brought retired slugger Willie Horton to the Yankees as a "Tranquility Coach."

The manager might as well delegate, because the truth about the profession is that a manager can barely influence the outcome of most games once they begin. Any baseball team is going to lose approximately fifty games and win the same amount, fairly convincingly— with or without a manager's input. On these occasions, the manager just stands in the dugout and practices his squint, or his chew, or spitting out sunflower seeds. It's what the manager does in the other sixty or so close games that tells his worth to a team. How many extra wins are a good manager's strategies worth? Ten wins would be a lot—the difference between an eighty-five-win third- or fourth-place finish and a possible pennant.

What makes a manager? It's no accident that so many of them seem to have been delivered from Central Casting, with the imperial, clear gaze of the peerless tactician, the regal bearing of the natural-born leader, or the shock of white hair to suggest wisdom and maturity. It's not just The Look that counts; without question the way a manager carries himself, day by day, sends a message to his ball club. In the high-pressure pinch, the manager tries not to appear as if his bladder and bowels are about to let go. Instead, by exuding the inner resolve to get the job done, he lends his players determination and confidence.

This is the genesis of the durable managers' basic expressions— Whitey Herzog's famous squint, his mouth somewhere between a grimace and a smile; Earl Weaver's ornery, feisty, combative look (when he wasn't puffing on a cigarette); Sparky Anderson's wide-eyed attentiveness; the pursed, businesslike lips of Tony LaRussa; or the calm, detached look that some managers favor, that faraway gaze into the middle distance.

When Bucky Dent was hired as Yankee manager, he provided a textbook lesson in how *not* to comport oneself in the dugout when your team is struggling. Indeed, there wasn't much Dent could do during the first two months of the 1990 season with a patchwork pitching staff and a lineup that couldn't score runs. Some veteran managers might have been able to feign serenity in the dugout, but Dent looked mortified. His dugout body language was a complete portfolio of horrible vibes. He would take off his cap and run his hand through his hair, or hold his hand over his mouth; at times he even shielded his eyes, as if he couldn't bear to watch what was transpiring on the field.

When things appear hopeless, it is the manager's role to emulate the genial captain of the *Titanic,* and instead of panicking, tell the passengers, "Ladies and gentlemen, not to worry. We're just taking on a little ice." Dent's comments to the press after losses were strict no-nos for managers, lines like, "I don't know what's happening out there, but it's been happening all year." Or, "I don't know what else I can do"; and, finally, the last-resort comment: "What can I say?"

Historically, managers get too much credit when they win, and too much blame when they lose. As Warren Spahn said about Casey Stengel as the losing manager of the Mets, "I knew him both before and after he was a genius." The deck trembles against the manager, because when he has a lousy team, he's called a lousy manager, and when he wins with a good team, the term is—"push-button manager."

It was said that Shirley Temple could have managed the Big Red Machine of the mid-'70s instead of Sparky Anderson, or led the frightening '61 Yankees instead of Ralph Houk, and still won pennants. Hey, maybe Ms. Temple wouldn't make a bad manager. I often think of late-inning baseball strategy in terms of just that conundrum—what would Shirley Temple do in this situation?

The truth is, it's the players who make the manager look good or bad most of the time. A manager is almost totally hamstrung by the character and ability of his team. What can the manager really do? Can he change the personality of any player? For the most part, the lazy ones remain lazy, the conscientious ones conscientious, and the ones who are not punctual, who don't practice, who take drugs, and get slapped with the occasional paternity suit—well, they generally can't be reformed without considerable professional help.

Neither can the manager change the basic level of ability of any player, although managers have tried to convince players that they're much better than they think they are. Sparky Anderson was one who would occasionally dust off a plaque in the Hall of Fame for some unproven rookie, or compare the rough-edged Kirk Gibson, fresh out of NCAA football, to Mickey Mantle. Sometimes pumping up the player to perform at a level he didn't know he could reach does work. But eventually the player comes down to earth, unable to maintain his new level of play.

Nobody in baseball can really put his finger on what makes a good manager. One of the things that organizations look for first is managing experience, preferably in the majors. For many teams, the search starts with finding a tried-and-true "baseball person." This weeds out a lot of candidates. Nothing looks better on a job résumé than another job managing a big-league team, even if that team finished dead last. This is how the same applicants get recycled, as happened in 1960 when the Indians and Tigers traded their managers—Jimmy Dykes for Joe Gordon.

Baseball has been run for a long time by men whose lives have been intersecting and intertwining for decades. The prime current example is Don Zimmer, who went to the same elementary school as best friend Jim Frey, the Cubs' general manager. After playing in the majors for the Dodgers, Cubs, Reds, and Senators, Zimmer managed the Padres, Red Sox, Rangers, and Cubs. It's a wonder there's anyone working in baseball, from executive to clubhouse attendant, who hasn't crossed paths with Don Zimmer.

It is called "the old-boy network." Blacks aren't getting the job offers because there are simply no blacks in the old-boy networks, and not because of the notion that blacks lack "some of the necessities," a statement made by Dodger executive Al Campanis on "Nightline" that more or less ended his usefulness to baseball.

Frank Robinson became the first black manager when he took over the Cleveland Indians in 1975. Few great players who became managers had ever come close to equaling their success as players. Sure, there were pennants won by Lou Boudreau and Joe Cronin, and Frank Robinson became a top-flight manager in Baltimore when he stopped expecting players to perform like Frank Robinson. But look at the baseball immortals who couldn't cut the mustard as the main man in the dugout—Ty Cobb, Tris Speaker, Ted Williams, Rogers Hornsby, Walter Johnson, Christy Mathewson, Mel Ott.

Most of the best managers have indeed come from the ranks of the marginal players. Whitey Herzog, Earl Weaver, Dick Williams, Sparky Anderson, Tony LaRussa, Jim Leyland—these were guys who played ball but didn't have the natural talent to hold down a big-league job. As Jim Palmer used to say about Weaver, "The only thing he knows about pitching is that he couldn't hit it." But some of the guys who struggled as ballplayers, who were forced to sit on the bench, watched and watched some more, asked questions, and *learned*. They got hooked on the games within the games.

Baseball has had its share of "interesting" managers—that is, men whose intellectual mobility was somewhat limited. As Jim Bouton said about Joe Schultz, who managed him when he was on the expansion Seattle Pilots, "Joe Schultz would have been a better manager if he understood more. Of course, if he understood more, he might not have been a manager." Sparky Anderson freely admitted, "You don't have to be a Harvard professor to manage baseball. In fact, I think you're better off having an IQ like mine."

When Maury Wills managed the Seattle Mariners in 1981, he put on some moves never before seen up in the biggies. Wills once held up a game for ten minutes while he searched for a pinch-hitter. When he found out he didn't have one, he tried to send up a player who'd already pinch-hit before in the game. Another time, he was asked who would be his center fielder and he replied, "I wouldn't be surprised if it was Leon Roberts." The writers were surprised; Roberts had been traded to Texas five weeks earlier. Wills's mishaps pointed up one of the most important rules for managers: always know who's on the roster.

Getting the Edge

There are no real secrets to managing, no arcane, magical, mystical strategies. The manager cannot devise special effects; all the strategic options in baseball are pretty basic, and stay that way. At the 1964 World Series, after the Yankees lost the first game to the Cards, sportswriters asked manager Yogi Berra what he was going to do differently for the next contest. Yogi just stared at the reporters. "There's no trick plays," he said in his inimitable deadpan. "This ain't football."

A modern manager like Tony LaRussa can study his computer printouts and pitcher-batter matchups, and consider all kinds of odds and percentages based on isolated player strengths and weaknesses. LaRussa has his coaches chart not only what hitters have done against every pitcher, but where they have put the ball in play against each type of pitch. The A's manager is convinced that such preparations help win games, but others remain inveterate hunch players. When Don Zimmer was asked why he made a move that went against the book, like calling for a hit and run with the bases loaded, the count full, and one out, he said, "What book? I ain't seen no friggin' book!"

The unpredictable manager may not have the odds on his side, but he does have the element of surprise. You could never be sure what Billy Martin was going to do. He might try to squeeze a run home with the bases loaded, or steal a base when you least expected it. Martin knew from his experience as an infielder that a moment of hesitation could be ruinous, so he always managed in this way, aggressively, to keep everybody out there on their toes.

"When Billy was managing in his prime," recalled Tony Kubek, "there wasn't a man who had a better feel for the game, the quality they call instinct for making the right move. Every manager says, 'I don't worry about what the other guy does, I just manage my talent, what I've got.' But with Billy, I think managers managed against him, and when they did that, he had every one of 'em.

"One example would be the year when he didn't have a very good team in Oakland in 1981. He had about four good position players [Rickey Henderson, Dwayne Murphy, Tony Armas, Cliff Johnson] and stacked them in the first four spots. In spring training in Arizona, I'll never forget, he hit and ran, double stole, he had 'em doing things that were incredible. And once the season started, all these advance scouts had their pitchers pitching out against him. The other managers were so on edge that they were managing against him, and for two months he had his hitters always hitting on 2–0 and 3–1, and got off to a terrific start. It was brilliant."

Most managers are more comfortable "going by the book." The Book may not be available in any library, but its golden rules are ingrained in the heads of managers. The Book says, "Never intentionally walk the winning run on base." This is why in 1951 Bobby Thomson wasn't walked before he hit the shot heard 'round the world. Willie Mays was on deck, a rookie whose knees were shaking. Plus Thomson had homered in an earlier game off Ralph Branca. Leo Durocher even gloated afterward about how Charlie Dressen blew the game by not walking Thomson. Dressen went by the book.

So did Sparky Anderson one day in Tiger Stadium. George Brett had already hit two homers in the game, and he came up in the ninth with a man on second and his team down by a run. Sparky pitched to him and Brett hit his third homer to win the game. The Book didn't have to take the heat; Sparky did.

In 1990 Sparky adopted the intentional pass as the way to go, walking Wade Boggs on purpose three times in one game. It worked. The Red Sox stranded eight runners after the walks. "It doesn't take a lot of sense," said Anderson after the game, "to figure out who to walk."

The Book says, "Play to tie at home but to win on the road." Earl Weaver thought that was nonsense. For him it depended on who was up in the batting order in the late innings. If his weak hitters were up in a road game, then Weaver figured he'd better try to get one run and take his chances when the home team came up to bat.

The Book says, "Give up the out with a man on second and no outs, hitting to the right side to get the runner to third so he can score on a fly ball." Again, Weaver insisted that it depended on who was at the plate. If it was a right-handed power hitter, Weaver didn't want the batter giving himself up when a home run was possible.

Today the mythical "Book" is bigger than ever in the high-tech '90s. There is an unprecedented wealth of information available. But what it comes down to is not how much information the teams can cull, but how they process it, and what conclusions they draw from it.

"Weaver isolated the important stats fifteen years ago," said Met executive Frank Cashen. "Every hitter versus every pitcher; hitters versus left- and right-handed pitching, recent streaks. When you go much beyond Earl you're just confusing yourself."

In one game in 1979, Weaver didn't have the stats on how the Orioles had done against a California pitcher named John Montague who entered the game in the late innings. After frantically riffling through game accounts, the stat man finally came up with the information, which he immediately called in to the dugout: John Lowenstein was 2–2 against Montague with a homer. Weaver inserted Lowenstein as a pinch-hitter, and he won the game with a three-run homer.

Even a manager who likes to play the percentages has to maintain some air of unpredictability and keep changing his patterns. The Book says that the ideal situation for the hit-and-run play is with a man on first, one out, and the count at two balls and one strike. Fine, but the other manager knows that's the ideal count as well, and the game of stratagems is on. If you hit and run on the 2–1 count all the time, the other teams, who are watching closely for everything you like to do, will start calling pitchouts on 2–1, and throw out your baserunners.

A manager might give the hit-and-run sign, then assume that the other manager has called for a pitchout; so the first manager will make a theatrical display of wiping off the hit-and-run sign. If he thinks the other manager has in turn called off the pitchout, then he might try slyly to put it on again. Even if the count is 2–0, the bold manager might not care about walking the hitter and still call for a pitchout if he's pretty sure that the runner is going and has a good chance to throw him out.

Eventually, after weighing all the pros and cons of a given baseball situation—the pitcher, the hitter, the baserunner, the score—he has to give the sign. The manager usually gives the signs to his third-base coach, but there are varying degrees of paranoia about how to do this and keep it a secret. Billy Martin would sometimes go through a whole bunch of signs as a decoy—it was the coach next to him who was giving the real signs. Dick Williams used to try to subvert the sign stealers by giving signs to his third-base coach a few pitches ahead of time, signs that his players weren't even aware of yet. One way of doing this was to flash signs when there was a foul ball or a base hit, when everyone supposedly was watching the ball.

A lot of managers today use these decoys, because in each opposing dugout there are baseball voyeurs trying to steal the signs. Today, stealing signs is considered by many to be an art form that requires patience and dedication. Nobody is more dedicated than White Sox coach Joe Nossek, who has built a reputation as the game's best code-breaker. Nossek actually videotapes all the opposing third-base coaches and then studies them for clues. Occasionally he informs an opposing manager that one of his players missed a sign the other day.

There is little honor among managers when it comes to stealing the other team's signals. When he was managing in Texas in 1974, Martin himself was accused of having a closed-circuit camera in the outfield: his coach, Jim Fregosi, was allegedly watching in the clubhouse, giving the catcher's signs to Martin by walkie-talkie. Martin carried a battery-pack transmitter in his back pocket and a microphone in his hand, and his base coaches had miniature receivers and earplugs so they could receive Martin's tips.

But you don't need electronic capabilities to steal and relay signs. At the old Polo Grounds, Leo Durocher once put a spy in center field who would raise and lower a venetian blind to indicate a fastball or curve to the Giant hitters. In Cleveland stolen signs used to be relayed to the hitters by moving the eyes of a painted Indian on the fence. The new electronic scoreboards may have made it a little more difficult to cheat in such quaint fashion.

Giants manager Roger Craig, who had an uncanny success rate for calling pitchouts and pickoffs when he was the Tiger pitching coach, says the players are the ones who frequently give away the signs. "When a play is on, the baserunners will try to set up differently and they tip it off. I didn't steal signs. I watched carefully. Habits. Body language. They'll tell you a lot."

Once a team gets burned a couple of times, they will change their signs, which is the ultimate victory for the sign-stealer. After a team changes its signals, you've got the players as well as the manager overthinking and being a little less loosey-goosey. Tony LaRussa and his Oakland coaching staff strike such fear into the opposition for their ability to steal signs that in the 1990 World Series the Reds' third-base coach Sam Perlozzo changed all the signs after the third game—even though the Reds had won all three.

A new set of signals can make it doubly hard for a manager to get his own players to pick up the signs, and some prefer to bypass all the chicanery and just put the play on. For more than a decade, Oriole manager Earl Weaver's squeeze sign was simply removing his cap. When Whitey Herzog was the Angels' third-base coach in the mid-1970s, he had trouble getting Mickey Rivers's attention so he could give him the steal sign. Finally, he came up with a foolproof signal. He would whistle, yell "Hey, Mick," and point toward second base. "If you're going to give a sign, the guy you're giving it to better be able to get it," explained Herzog. "They hardly ever threw Mick out anyway."

A good manager looks for any edge he can get, and if he can't find one, he often looks for ways to create one. When Eddie Stanky managed the Chicago White Sox in the '60s, they were a fast team with no power, and Stanky was frequently accused of storing game balls in a freezer to deaden the insides since his team wasn't going to hit any homers anyway. A few years later, catcher Jerry McNertney admitted that Stanky was indeed pulling the frozen-ball trick. The "refrigerator ball" would be taken out of the freezer a few hours before a game, so the surface would warm up while the core of the baseball remained frozen. When a batter hit the ball it would make a curious *splat!* sound and just die in the outfield.

When Stanky played second base for the New York Giants in the '50s, he used to jump in the air and wave his arms to distract the batter. This caused the adoption of a new rule, which forever forbade Stanky and his ilk to do this. Stanky's keystone partner at shortstop was Alvin Dark, who also, as a manager, bent the rules to his advantage. (Perhaps it was just another amazing coincidence that they both played under the all-time rule-bender, Leo Durocher.) Dark was managing the San Francisco Giants in 1962 and his team was involved in a tight pennant race with the Dodgers; that was the year that Maury Wills stole 104 bases. When the Dodgers came into San Francisco late in the season, Dark ordered the groundskeeper to flood the area around first base. By game time it was like quicksand. The umpires ordered that dirt be poured around the base, but it just turned everything to mud. Wills didn't steal a base that night, the Giants swept the Series, and wound up in the World Series.

On those ballfields that do not have artificial turf, it's the manager, not the groundskeeper, who determines the length of the infield grass. Teams with slow fielders want the grass high so the ball will slow down, just as teams with sinker-ball pitchers want it high as well, to knock down all those grounders. When Earl Weaver took over the Orioles, the grass was tall, and the Orioles' super infielders, like Brooks Robinson and Mark Belanger, made all the plays look easy. The trouble was, the other teams, aided by the jungle overgrowth, were diving and making all kinds of great plays. So Weaver had the groundskeeper cut the grass down to a nub. Immediately, the quick-zipping grounders skipped just out of the reach of the lesser fielders on the other teams, but not out of reach of Belanger and Robinson and company. *Voilà!*

Managing at its purest most often takes place before the game. Earl Weaver thought that choosing his lineup and making his batting order were among the key decisions of baseball. It is here that a manager reveals much of his baseball personality. Does he choose his starters because of their offensive skills or their defensive skills? If he likes offense, what kind of offensive player—a guy who can hit the ball nine miles, or a guy who can get on base and steal bases? Will he take a chance on a young player, even when others don't think he's quite ready? How does he adjust to what the opposition is throwing at him, especially the starting pitcher?

After a manager figures out where everybody is supposed to play, he is still faced with the question of what batting order is going to produce the most runs. This is one of the fields of baseball inquiry that for years was ruled by knee-jerk, habitual stupidity. Why else would managers repeatedly put a scrappy second baseman at the top of the batting order, no matter how low his batting average and on-base percentage was? That's what managers did out of nothing more than pure inertia, even though it crippled a team's run production.

As manager of the '61 Yankees, Ralph Houk installed second baseman Bobby Richardson in the leadoff spot to get on base in front of Maris, Mantle, Berra, Howard, and Skowron, and this choice cost the Yankees a bundle of runs. Richardson played in 162 games, with an on-base average of .293, and scored the paltry total of eighty runs while hitting in front of one of the most fearsome lineups ever. Elston Howard, who had an on-base percentage of .387 that year, would have been their best leadoff man, but Howard was disqualified by being a catcher. Richardson qualified even though he wasn't all that scrappy, being a devout Christian—but he was a second baseman.

This quaint notion was slowly overturned by a few pioneering leadoff men in the '70s, such as Bobby Bonds, an outfielder who drew a lot of walks, stole a lot of bases, and hit doubles to put himself in scoring position. Within the next decade, baseball had a new prototype leadoff man, premier players like Rickey Henderson and Tim Raines, who had speed and could hit for high average as well as steal bases.

The team a manager puts together is most effective if it is tailored to the home park in which it will play half of its games. The best managers even go so far as to acquire specific kinds of players to fit the home stadium. Look, for example, at the St. Louis Cardinals team that Whitey Herzog put together in the '80s when he wore the dual hats of manager and general manager. To fit the huge dimensions and artificial turf of Busch Stadium, Herzog developed the Go-Go Cards, speedy, contact switch-hitters. Herzog didn't always favor that kind of team, not when he managed in Kansas City, where it was far easier to hit home runs. But in a park like Busch Stadium, speed enabled the outfielders to cut balls off before they got through the gaps; and an offense built around the stolen base is the most reliable weapon when the power alleys are 390 feet away. Herzog's tailor-made Cardinal ball club went to the World Series three times in the 1980s. The great Yankee dynasties were assembled by accenting left-handed pull hitters who could take advantage of the shorter right-field fence. First it was Ruth and Gehrig; then, in the early '60s, Maris, Mantle, Berra; and in the late '70s, Reggie Jackson, Chris Chambliss, and Graig Nettles.

Other ballparks call for more subtle player adjustments. In Wrigley Field, for instance, where the wind can turn routine fly balls into home runs, should the manager seek pitchers capable of getting ground-ball outs? Then there is the problem of the team built for its home park when it goes on the road. The Red Sox are the best example. The Sox tended to stock their team with power hitters who could reach Fenway Park's Green Monster in left field. More often than not, they wound up with a slow-footed club that couldn't get on base away from home. The power-laden 1977 Sox hit 213 home runs and were typically slow afoot. Over the years the Red Sox strategy always ignored one other factor—pitching. The Sox seldom built a great pitching staff, possibly because of their intense concentration on developing *sluggers*. And in Fenway park left-handed pitchers became, and still are, an endangered species. Pitching may not be 75 percent of baseball as some claim, but *balance* is still the name of the game.

One philosophy managers do rely on today is the platooning of players. At its best, a platoon combination like the one Earl Weaver employed at Baltimore in left field in 1983—using the left-handed John Lowenstein and the right-handed Gary Roenicke—put up the best statistics of any left-fielder in the league. Both played a little over one hundred games in the outfield. Lowenstein had fifteen homers and sixty RBIs and Roenicke had nineteen homers and sixty-four RBIs.

Platooning has been around since early in the century, but it was Casey Stengel who brought it to an art form beginning in 1949. Injuries that year forced Stengel into using platoon combinations at several positions, but then he adopted it as his intended style, acquiring in subsequent years a bunch of infielders—Bobby Brown, Jerry Coleman, Jerry Lumpe, Gil McDougald—who could play third, short, and second. When Stengel was trailing in a game, he could fearlessly pinch-hit for his infielders, knowing he had replacements. Then he could insert players depending on whether he was going for offense or defense.

Replacing two players at once allowed him to juggle the batting order, so that the better hitter could come up sooner. Today it's used most frequently in the National League (pitchers *bat* in the NL) to "hide" a new pitcher's spot in the batting order by inserting a second player into the lineup, perhaps one who already pinch-hit that inning. This move, known as the "double switch," is now rather commonplace in the National League but it was Stengel who set the trend.

The manager's game is played at every level in baseball, not just the majors. No better example can be shown than the one involving Clint Courtney and Jim Bunning. They were different types of people, to say the least. Bunning was a hard-throwing pitcher who later became a Republican congressman. Courtney, nicknamed "Scrap Iron," was a brawler who was rumored to have once eaten a jockstrap full of rusty nails. When he was a catcher on the St. Louis Browns, he had to be asked by his teammates to stop causing bench-clearing brawls every series. That was because Courtney had this habit on any tag play at the plate of bashing the runner on his temple, hard enough so you could see the stitches imprinted on the guy's head. He was the same way as a manager.

Warner Fusselle, currently host of "Major League Baseball Magazine" on ESPN, was then announcing for the Richmond Braves. "Courtney and Bunning hated each other," he told me. "I think it had something to do with Courtney having a streak of not striking out and Bunning striking him out after two hundred at-bats. So they were both managing in the International League, Bunning with Toledo, the Phillies farm club, and Courtney with Richmond. Every time Richmond played Toledo, the strangest things in the world would happen, and Richmond would always win. There was no way they were supposed to win, but somehow Courtney would always win.

"One night early in the year it was rainy and cold and Toledo was winning seven–two in the sixth inning. Two hundred people waited out a delay for an hour, then they resumed the game. The Braves got a run in the seventh, another in the eighth, then all of a sudden it's the ninth inning and the Braves are down seven–four. They score a run and get a couple of guys on base with two outs, and the batter is Dale Soderholm, brother of major leaguer Eric Soderholm. Soderholm takes two balls, and then Courtney comes running out of the dugout and signals down to the bullpen for the catcher, Jim 'Bobo' Breazeale, to come and pinch-hit for Soderholm.

"Bobo comes running in, he's got a bad leg, he doesn't even know what's going on. But he hits his first pitch for a game-winning three-run homer, and the Braves win, eight–seven. After the game, everyone's going up to Courtney, asking, 'Hey, Scraps, how did you know to make that move?' 'Sheet,' he said, 'I've got the best fastball hitter in the minor leagues on the bench, I know he's gonna get a fastball on two–oh and I knew he'd hit it out.'

"One time we're in Toledo and Richmond had a young pitcher named Frank LaCorte who had a great arm but no control. In the fourth inning he walks the bases loaded, and then Courtney goes out to talk to him. He goes three–oh on the next batter, and Courtney goes out to remove him. He starts screaming at LaCorte in the dugout that he doesn't want to see him again: 'You can't pitch, you're off this team, you're getting sent down to Savannah.' Meanwhile, Bunning comes out and argues that Courtney just went out to the mound twice during the same batter—he can't take LaCorte out of the game, he has to finish pitching to that batter! Technically, Courtney was not allowed to come out to the mound a second time during the same batter. So LaCorte goes back out to the mound, after being aired out and sent down to Savannah, and the batter bunts on a three–oh pitch and pops into a double play. He gets the next batter and gets out of it, so it's still nothing–nothing.

"The pitcher for Toledo has a no-hitter, and the game goes extra innings, with LaCorte still pitching a shutout. Soderholm got on first base and Ivan Murrell, who was lame, hit one off the wall, and Richmond won one–nothing as Murrell barely made it to first base. So here was a game where the Richmond pitcher was on his way to the low minors, and the Toledo pitcher threw a no-hitter, and Courtney still beat Bunning.

"We go to Toledo for another game, and a very similar type thing happened. Bunning got ejected in the sixth inning. In the late innings, with Pablo Torrealba pitching, Courtney went out to the mound, then went out to the catcher and told the catcher to tell Torrealba something. When the Toledo writers told Bunning what had happened, he said, 'That's illegal!,' so he protested the game, even though it was already over and Bunning wasn't even there when it happened.

"That was a Saturday night. On Sunday the team drove to Rochester. In the back room of the hotel there's a Ping-Pong table. Preston Hanna is playing Ping-Pong with Mickey Mahler, and Courtney is sitting over by the window. He suddenly passes out, his head hits the window, and he's taken to the hospital. I say, 'We really need Scraps for this three-game series,' and Hanna says it happened to his father one time and he was laid up for a week in the hospital.

"I called the hospital around midnight, and they finally put coach Dirty Al Gallagher on the phone. 'Hey, Dirty Man, how's Scraps?' And the Dirty Man said, 'He died thirty minutes ago of a heart attack. Get everybody together, tell the team.' Everybody was in total shock. The players didn't want to play. But they had sold nine thousand tickets.

"Bob Lemon came in to manage, Dirty Man was in the third-base coaching box, and they hung Courtney's uniform up in the dugout. A month later, George Sisler, the league president, upholds the earlier protest by Bunning, and they have to play the last out all over again. So in August we're supposed to play three doubleheaders in a row in Toledo, because we had this spell where we got rained out ten days in a row. Before the first doubleheader, we replayed the protest game. We never got the last out, and Toledo won the ballgame.

"The irony was that Bunning finally beat him, but only after Scraps Courtney had been dead for a month."

Handling Players

Imagine Mike Ditka chewing out a Chicago Bears player on the sidelines while himself wearing shoulder pads and a helmet. Or Chuck Daly, his hair perfectly coiffed, wearing a Pistons uniform and high-top sneakers. It would look ridiculous. And yet the baseball manager sports a full uniform, spikes, and his team's cap. It wasn't always that way. In the early days of baseball, the manager was sometimes set off from the players by his three-piece suits and high starched collars. Connie Mack used to sit in the Philadelphia A's dugout dressed as if attending a board meeting of U.S. Steel, no matter if it was a ninety-five-degree afternoon. Mack preferred not to wear a uniform. There was no rule against it as long as he stayed in the dugout; he was just forbidden from ever stepping on the field. Mack may have discovered some magic elixir; in formal attire, he managed into his nineties.

Today's baseball managers don't live so long; might be because even though they dress like their boys, they're definitely not one of the boys. The manager, as his name implies, represents *management*, the overall needs of the organization, and sentiment seldom enters into the equation. Nobody makes the starting lineup because of a sunny disposition or manifold contributions to charity. A manager has to be careful about getting too close to his players. "I might have to send a guy down," Earl Weaver once said, "and that's hard enough without being friends with them." The only possible exception is the guy the manager knows he isn't going to have to cut or trade, like the close friendship and mutual admiration society that developed between George Brett and Whitey Herzog in Kansas City.

There are good reasons why Leo Durocher entitled his autobiography *Nice Guys Finish Last*. A Nice Guy is not going to coldly exploit the insecurities of his players, threatening them with banishment to some Albanian salt mine if they don't give him their best effort. Nice guys don't pull the carpet out from under veterans as soon as they can't cut it. Durocher was not a nice-guy manager, but Gene Mauch found the most difficult task he had was "telling a guy that, in your opinion, he can't play in the big leagues anymore."

A manager, in short, doesn't expect friendship from his players, but he demands respect. All a manager can do is try to get his players to bust their butts for him. In June 1990, Jim Leyland had his Pirates in first place but he still knew that his leadership of the ball club hung on a factor that he really had no control over. "There will come a day," he said, "when, for whatever reason, these players will decide that they don't want to play hard for me anymore, and they'll quit on me. On that day, I'll be gone. It's as simple as that, and I'm not dumb enough to think any different."

One of the things it comes down to is the match of personalities between a manager and a team. There are different kinds of teams, just as there are different kinds of managers. A young team lacking experience may need a teacher. A veteran team that's been through tough pennant races has often played its best under a low-keyed, *laissez-faire* manager, like Mayo Smith with the '68 Tigers or Harvey Kuenn with the '82 Brewers. Both of those clubs went to the World Series. Likewise, an underachieving team might fulfill its talents under a disciplinarian, but then fall into its old ways after the glow of winning has worn off. Teams are evolving all the time, and the right manager for one year may not be the right manager for the next.

Billy Martin was a perfect example of a manager who could goad a team to win big in his first season, with ever-diminishing returns in subsequent years. Martin won pennants with very different kinds of teams—an underachieving team in Minnesota, a close-to-over-the-hill veteran ball club in Detroit, a collection of highly paid, warring superegos in New York, and a very young team in Oakland. He forced his teams to adapt to his style by the sheer force of his personality, but his inflexibility may have been one of the reasons why he wore out his welcome so quickly in so many cities.

Martin never fretted much about how to handle players. "I don't believe in talking to my players when they're in a slump, and I don't believe in talking to my players when they're hitting." Presumably he didn't have time to be a handler of men because he had his hands full handling himself, but he would generally wind up with half the team in his corner, and the other half hating his guts.

When players started making big salaries, it changed the manager-player relationship, but Martin never changed; he would not baby his players. As a result, he got in fights with pitcher Dave Boswell in Minnesota, Reggie Jackson in New York, and pitcher Ed Whitson in a later stint managing the Yankees. Martin always thought that certain players were trying to undermine him and was always looking for spies in the clubhouse. As Martin's longtime buddy Mickey Mantle put it, "I always said Billy was the only guy who could hear someone giving him the finger." For Martin, winning was never enough.

To the old-line managers like Martin, the new breed of better-educated and better-paid players seemed less dedicated and tougher to discipline. Fining a player who makes a million a year is a futile exercise, and yet some managers insisted that was the only way to run a ball club. In 1980 Dallas Green took over the Phillies with the attitude that there was a new sheriff in town. His rules were formally printed up and issued to each player. The code established a curfew, set dress standards, limited drinking and card playing, imposed rigorous rules of conduct at practices, and banned players' children from the dugout during practices. Green won the division that year but two years later was gone.

The problem with Green was that he was managing as if in an earlier era. Beginning in the '70s, when spiraling player salaries first began to resemble those of rock stars, ballplayers' off-field behavior changed in kind. Big money, celebrity status, and high pressure were among the factors that led some players to cocaine, which was then considered by many as a recreational nonaddictive drug. Nobody knows how many players indulged, but it was enough of a problem for it to culminate in the highly publicized trial in Pittsburgh of two drug dealers in the fall of 1985. Seven major leaguers (six still active) were called as witnesses, and seventeen players in all were named in the testimonies as having used cocaine in the late '70s and early '80s.

Was the permissive, live-and-let-live approach of the managers at fault? When Pirate manager Chuck Tanner took the stand, he said he was not aware that there were drugs in the clubhouse. The judge ripped him apart for that admission. How oblivious did Tanner claim to be? Well, he didn't notice that accused player Curtis Strange, a fixture in his clubhouse, was servicing much of the team with cocaine.

In defense of Tanner, drug abuse does present a difficult problem for a manager. A manager can't smell coke on a player's breath. When Steve Howe was a Dodger pitcher from 1980 to 1985, Tommy Lasorda couldn't detect Howe's repeated relapses of cocaine use. "At first I couldn't see it," Lasorda recalled. While Lasorda did notice a personality change, he said he assumed it was from the rigors of the season. "There were telltale signs there, but we were not too knowledgeable about it back then."

Cocaine's impact on player performance is also virtually impossible to judge on a short-term basis. For a time, cocaine use might even *aid* performance. Look at what the '82 Cardinals did with three key players who admitted to using coke—Joaquin Andujar, Keith Hernandez, and Lonnie Smith: they won the World Series.

Eventually Whitey Herzog weeded these players from his team. Herzog always demanded a certain level of responsibility from his players. In one celebrated incident in 1979, he dragged Garry Templeton into the dugout after Templeton had made an obscene gesture at the fans in St. Louis. In a strong show of authority, he fined, suspended, chastised, and finally traded the talented Templeton. "Somebody in our society has to draw the line somewhere," he said, "and I'm drawing it here."

Discipline is not the approach that builds winners, however. It is leadership and the ability to motivate players. If the players believe in the manager, they will walk through that wall of fire with confidence, sure that they will succeed.

The best example of a manager for these times may be Tommy Lasorda. In the 1989 World Series he called for the hit and run fifteen times, and Dodger batters amazingly got eleven hits on those pitches. As an underdog, Lasorda had the opportunity to dig deep into his bag of classic motivational psychology. He saw a perfect opening before one Series game with Oakland when Bob Costas said on NBC's pregame show that the injury-riddled Dodger lineup, minus Mike Marshall and Kirk Gibson, and with Pedro Guerrero traded away, was possibly the worst-hitting team in Series history. Lasorda told his team to go out and show them, and they did.

Lasorda has plenty of critics. His fondness for hugging his players has earned the Dodgers the derogatory nickname of "the Happiness Boys." He likes to keep his team loose, and makes sure to always have a club prankster on the roster, a Jay Johnstone or Rick Dempsey, Mickey Hatcher, and their fellow "Stunt Men." "Lasorda," wrote Tom Boswell, "raises a disturbing question. Is a manager above all a glorified cruise director whose central function is to establish and maintain a club's day-to-day tone?" Bill James insists that the front office really runs the Dodgers. "Lasorda just signs the lineup card and entertains the reporters."

Lasorda does indeed seem more interested in celebrity hobnobbing in Los Angeles than in the analysis of baseball statistics. As a raconteur and repository of endless one-liners, he keeps 'em laughin'. But most of all, he wins, sometimes with a team that would appear to be outclassed.

Before Lasorda, Walter Alston managed the Dodgers from 1954 to 1976, under twenty-three consecutive one-year contracts. He was Manager of the Year six times, and won over 2,000 games, including four world championships. Through it all, he was the strong and silent statesman, a stabilizing, if humorless, force. "I never copied another manager," he once said. "I realized you have to manage according to your own emotional and physical makeup." While he was known as a patient man, Alston was not afraid to challenge his players. One day early in the 1955 season, Don Newcombe balked at pitching batting practice, and Alston told him to turn in his uniform. They made peace the next day and Newk went on to post a 20–5 record in Brooklyn's only championship season.

Just as people wondered how Alston could ever follow the colorful managers who came before him, like Durocher and Charley Dressen, many questioned how Lasorda could live up to Alston's legacy of winning. But they don't anymore. Lasorda doesn't mind being corny about "bleeding Dodger blue," and doesn't care about playing the buffoon, but his public image is a far cry from the way he actually handles game situations. Here, from a World Series on-field mike, is the fourth game of the 1977 World Series. Pitcher Doug Rau has just given up three straight hits in the second inning, and the Yankees lead 1–0. Lasorda comes to the mound, knowing that he is miked.

RAU: I feel good, Tommy.

LASORDA: I don't give a shit you feel good—there's four mother-fucking hits up there.

RAU: They're all fucking hits the opposite way.

LASORDA: I don't give a fuck.

RAU: I got a left-handed hitter. I can strike this motherfucker out.

LASORDA: I don't give a shit, Dougie.

RAU: I think you're wrong.

LASORDA: I may be wrong, but that's my goddamn job. I—

RAU: I ain't fucking hurting.

LASORDA: I'll make the fucking decisions here. Okay?

RAU: You let three runs get up on the fucking board yesterday.

LASORDA: I don't give a fuck.

RAU: Hey, Tommy—

LASORDA: DON'T GIVE ME ANY SHIT, GODDAMN IT! I'll make the fucking decisions. Keep your fucking mouth shut, I told ya.

RAU: If I didn't feel good, I wouldn't say anything.

LASORDA: I don't give a shit, Doug. I'm the fucking manager of the fucking team. I got to make the fucking decisions, and I'll make them to the fucking best of my ability.

[Pitcher Rick Rhoden is announced and comes in from the bullpen while the organist plays a jaunty tune.]

LASORDA: It may be the fucking wrong decision, but I'll make it. Don't worry about it. I'll make the fucking decision. I gave you a fucking chance to walk out of here. I can't fuck around—we're down two games to one. If it was yesterday, that's a different fucking story.

RAU: There's a left-handed hitter coming up, what about that?

LASORDA: I DON'T GIVE A SHIT! You got three, three left-handed hitters, and they all got fucking hits on ya. Whoever that is, Jackson

Al Kaline being led off the field at Yankee Stadium in 1962 after breaking his collarbone making a game-saving catch with two out in the ninth inning.

Good ol' boy Hugh Casey, said his manager Leo Durocher, had all the guts in the world. But once upon a time, he froze in a big-game situation while pitching against the Yankees in the 1941 World Series. After his playing career ended, he wound up taking his own life.

According to his agent, David Pinter, it was the home run Donnie Moore (above) gave up to Dave Henderson of the Red Sox in the 1986 ALCS that led to his suicide. "He never got over it."

Moments of triumph for relievers are often short-lived. Within days after closing out the 1988 ALCS win against the Red Sox, Dennis Eckersley gave up a game-winning home run to Kirk Gibson in the World Series that he dreamed about for six months afterward.

There was ample evidence before the fateful game six of the '86 World Series that Bill Buckner's injuries ware causing him to struggle in the field. Still, Red Sox manager John McNamara left him in the game, and he let Mookie Wilson's grounder go through his aching legs.

A shattered Ralph Branca after giving up the shot heard 'round the world to Bobby Thomson, probably the most famous home run in baseball history.

After the ornery submarine pitcher Carl Mays (left) of the New York Giants hit and killed Ray Chapman (right) of the Indians with a pitch in 1920, baseball instituted the practice of throwing out dirty, hard-to-see balls.

The batter's last recourse, charging the mound. Here Reggie Jackson goes after John Denny of the Indians in 1981.

Two intimidating National League pitchers who thrived in the brushback era of the '60s were Don Drysdayle (left) and Bob Gibson (right). "If I wanted to hit a guy, I hit him," said Gibson, "but I never aimed at the head."

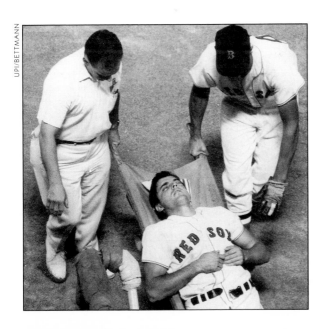

Tony Conigliaro, the youngest home run champ in AL history, had his career derailed after being hit by a pitch in 1967.

The great Lefty Grove, who finished his career with the Red Sox, practiced a fork ball on the sidelines for years before using it in a crucial game situation.

Gaylord Perry (above) liked to keep opposing hitters guessing as to whether he was greasing the ball to throw illegal pitches, at least faking that he was loading up before every delivery. "I tried everything on the old horsehide except for chocolate sauce toppin'."

When notorious streak hitter Jack Clark is in a slump, no one is safe from flying batting helmets.

Keith Hernandez made himself a master of the games within the game. "Baseball," he said, "is my meditation."

All-time homer king Hank Aaron (below) had such quick wrists that he always looked for the curveball because no pitcher, he claimed, could throw a fastball past him.

Casey Stengel, shown here clowning with pitcher Roger Craig of the woeful '62 Mets. To say the least, losing is no longer fun for New York's National League franchise.

and that fucking other guy. They all bat, they all hit, that guy that just hit the ball was a left-hander, wasn't he?

RAU: I jammed him. You know, the inside part of the plate—

LASORDA: I don't give a shit if you jammed him or not, he didn't get out. I can't let you out there in a fucking game like this. I got a fucking job to do. What's the matter with you?

[The Dodgers lose the game 4–2, and lose the Series in six games.]

There are several things that the manager looks for before deciding to give a pitcher the hook. One, a real attention-getter, is when pop-gun hitters start pulling the ball with authority. The manager will ask the pitching coach if the pitcher's delivery looks awkward. Another is when the pitcher starts to throw the ball high in the strike zone, which is frequently a result of fatigue. Also, a pitcher walking the leadoff man is a real signal that he's losing it, fast. And when a pitcher starts to lose it, he'll take more and more time between pitches, rubbing up the ball, wiping his brow, hitching his pants, or tying his shoes. This kind of body language means he really doesn't want to throw the ball to the next hitter; it's a cry to the manager to get him into a hot shower.

There are various ways to deal with the situation. Often, the manager will have the pitching coach talk to the pitcher, because the pitcher doesn't have to be removed until the second trip to the mound. Other times, when the manager isn't sure if he should take the pitcher out, he goes to the mound himself to ask the pitcher and catcher what he's got left. In the key late-inning situations, it's sometimes not sufficient for the pitcher to insist he's not tired. What the manager likes to hear is something more along these lines: "This bleeping guy is mine! I want him!"

Sometimes early in the season a manager will leave a pitcher in the game because he's trying to establish him for the long haul. "It's very important," said Dallas Green, "to prepare the pitching staff, not for April and May, but for September and October. You make your decisions to take ten pitchers, and you'd better use ten pitchers. Anybody can run a hot hand out there." As Earl Weaver said in his famous line about the Job-like patience he has demonstrated with some pitchers: "I gave Mike Cuellar more chances than I gave my first wife."

Weaver had one of baseball's great love-hate relationships with the ace of his staff, Jim Palmer. They were always arguing, sometimes good-naturedly, sometimes not. Palmer was fond of pointing out that all Weaver knew about pitching was that he couldn't hit it. But Palmer also conceded that Weaver's insistence on perfection, year after year, probably pushed him to have a Hall of Fame–caliber career. Ultimately, they had great respect for each other, even as they fussed, fumed, and feuded.

Oddly enough, a big part of Weaver's problem with Jim Palmer was that he refused to take Palmer *out* of games. Palmer would arm himself with statistics showing how much better a pitcher he was through the seventh inning, and thought his variety of ailments would only allow him to throw a certain number of pitches. But Weaver wanted Palmer to stay in games in the eighth inning, thinking that Palmer's problems with his rotor cuff or ulnar nerve were mostly in the pitcher's head. "When I wanted to leave Jim Palmer in," Weaver said, "he wanted out. When I wanted him out, he wanted to stay in." At the midpoint of his career in 1975, Palmer pitched twenty-five complete games, more than he completed from 1979 to 1984 combined.

Yankee left-hander Whitey Ford was frequently criticized by fans and press alike in 1961 for leaving games when Stengel would pull him in favor of reliever Luis Arroyo, whose screwball was close to untouchable that season. But Ford went 25–4 with that strategy. In fact, Arroyo saved only seven of Ford's victories that year. Ford's thirteen complete games that season would have led the major leagues in 1990, an indication of just how much pitching philosophy has changed. Even a quality starter today has little chance of staying in the game once the lead run comes to the plate in the late innings.

The use of relief pitching is now a science in baseball. The relievers are specialists—flamethrowers or guys with a nasty trick pitch. Most contemporary managers put their bullpen crew together in a strict pecking order. There are middle men to pitch the fifth and sixth innings; setup men to pitch the seventh and eighth; and closers to pitch the ninth. The Cincinnati Reds had the best bullpen in baseball in 1990, with Norm Charlton, Rob Dibble, and Randy Myers. When the lockout shortened spring training, many starters were not able to go deep into a game early in the year. It was no accident that manager Lou Piniella was able to use the best relievers in the league and get his team off to a tremendous start. In a tight game, Piniella would send out Charlton, then Dibble, then Myers. By knowing just when they were supposed to come into the game, the relievers could avoid something they absolutely hated, which was warming up without coming into the game; so they'd get their juices flowing at the right time.

The role of the setup man was solidified by the success that Yankee manager Bob Lemon had using Ron Davis to set up Gossage as the closer in the late '70s. Rob Dibble, however, was unhappy with saving only ten games or so a season, while he watched pitchers with half his stuff saving thirty games and making millions. Although Dibble had been among the most dominant pitchers in baseball for the last two years, Piniella established Randy Myers as the closer in 1990. Myers is a lefty and Dibble a righty, so a manager could utilize them as co-closers depending on the situation, but Piniella chose not to do so. The way he handled them was effective, as Myers and Dibble were co-MVPs of the Reds' victory over the Pirates in the playoffs, with neither giving up so much as a single run. In 1991, Piniella tabbed Dibble as the closer who got all the saves.

The bullpen-by-committee (using several different relievers to close games) can work well also, and in fact Jim Leyland employed that strategy for the Pirates in 1990 and won with it. There are advantages to spreading around the work of closing the wins. For one thing, it takes pressure off the relievers, who might have a bad game or two but don't have to worry about blowing the whole season for the ball club. And spreading the work around gives the other manager something else to think about; he doesn't know who he might face in the ninth inning.

Of course, how a manager handles his pitching staff changes with the context. If he's in a pennant race, he stops using the pitchers who haven't been effective and lets them do crossword puzzles in the bullpen. And if a manager doesn't have a long-term contract, he's a lot more liable to "ride the horses," pitch his best arms, even if he's in last place. Many teams that aren't perennial contenders play a game of revolving managers, so it has a crucial bearing on a manager's decisions.

Take Russ Nixon, manager of the Atlanta Braves, who had to feel that his job was in jeopardy in 1989 with his team again mired in dead last and the front office waffling about his future. Nixon had a young ace, John Smoltz, who burned up the National League in the first half of the season. But Smoltz developed a tear in the fatty pad of his elbow and reason dictated that he should just rest it, since the Braves were going to finish last anyway. But Nixon's job was in jeopardy, and so he continued starting Smoltz, and Smoltz started getting hammered. After Nixon signed a contract for the following season, he took no more risks with Smoltz.

This is not to say that the Braves' front office made Nixon feel totally secure. They surrounded him with ex-managers as coaches, instructors, and roving scouts, including Bobby Wine, Pat Corrales, Frank Howard, and GM Bobby Cox. Even Phil Niekro was buzzing around, saying, after the Braves got off to a 2–13 start, that he would like to manage someday.

When the Braves finally fired Russ Nixon in June 1990 the decision was one of the worst-kept secrets in baseball. Nixon said he knew he was going to be fired as early as the previous December when the National League managers assembled at the winter meetings in Nashville. As they prepared to take the annual group picture, the managers were jostling each other, trying to get away from Tommy Lasorda, because whoever had been to the right of Lasorda in the picture for the previous three years had lost his job—Chuck Tanner, Hal Lanier, and then Pete Rose. Nixon finally volunteered to stand next to him. "Ah, what the hell," he said, "I'm already gone."

How to Argue with Umpires

All in all, a manager would prefer to devote less time to fighting with his players, so he would then have more time and energy to fight with the umpires. These battles take place for a host of reasons, from blown calls to rule discrepancies to just plain personal vendettas. When an umpire misses a call and is honest about blowing it, a manager can't really ask for anything more; he knows he'll get the nod on the next close one, and he respects an umpire who admits he made a mistake. So sometimes the manager knows he's going to lose the argument, but win the war on the next call, especially if his team is at home.

What really lights a manager's short fuse is when an umpire is out of position and doesn't see the play, and still belligerently insists he made the right call. In that case, some managers will go at it until they have to be tossed. Sparky Anderson, for one. "I argue very little now," Anderson said. "I'll bet you I haven't been run out twice in four years. I used to be a wild man. When I started, I always felt like I was getting screwed. Well, they're not out to screw you. Oh, they might miss a play, but they're not doing it on purpose." (It wasn't the umpires that did Sparky in during the 1989 season, but the Tigers' last-place performance, which wore him down until he had to convalesce from stress and nervous exhaustion.)

The calls that umpires miss the most are on balls and strikes. "When you work the plate and call as many pitches as we do," said umpire John Kibler, "you're certainly going to miss some, because we're all human—and because players are human, they're gonna miss pitches, too. When you miss one, you know you're gonna get hollered at, and when you're an umpire, no matter what you do, someone's gonna holler at you."

Umpires love a pitcher like Catfish Hunter, who had great control and didn't argue on ball and strike calls. A pitcher like that gets the borderline calls, whereas the rookie pitcher still has to prove himself before the plate umpire will give him a strike on the same pitch. Within any game is the effort to sell the umpire on a pitch in the early innings, and then gradually push it as far as possible.

Frequently a manager's tirade is designed not so much to purge his own fury as to keep his players from being thrown out of the game. A manager would always prefer to get ejected himself. He doesn't have to pick up a bat to win the ballgame, and he can always manage the rest of the game from the runway or clubhouse if need be.

California Angels manager Doug Rader was a master at diffusing an argument; he would rush between an irate player and an increasingly agitated umpire and tell the ump that he was absolutely "the swellest guy I've ever known." On the other hand, a manager has to stick up for his players, as Tommy Lasorda acknowledged. "If my player thinks he's safe and he stands out there and argues and I'm sitting in there on my ass, that sure as hell don't look good. He's gonna say, 'What the hell's going on? I'm out here arguing and this guy's not saying anything.' "

It's expected of a manager to do a little finger-pointing and hell-raising with the umps. When Steve Boros, a very smart baseball man, wouldn't change his mild-mannered attitude while managing the Oakland A's, he was fired.

A shrewd manager knows that a strenuous argument when his team is getting blown out can sometimes deflect attention from how lousy his players have performed. The next day in the sports pages, the story is about the manager who went bananas, instead of the infielders who couldn't pick up the ball even if it had handles on it. It may have no bearing on the ballgame, but a good argument can purge a lot of frustrations, and revitalize the whole team.

Leo Durocher prided himself on being a great umpire-baiter and hater. In those days the foul line used to be laid down with white lime, so Leo the Lip, in addition to giving an umpire a tongue-lashing, would kick lime from the foul lines on the ump's pants so it would burn a hole in the fabric.

Umpires of Durocher's era would generally allow a manager to give him a good beef on a controversial call. One day Leo's Dodgers were trying to complete a double play when shortstop Pee Wee Reese dropped the ball as he was transferring it to his throwing hand. The second-base umpire had called the runner out, but then Reds manager Bill McKechnie came out and got the ump to consult with the tall, magisterial George Magerkurth, who was umpiring at third base. The next thing Durocher knew, everybody was safe. Durocher came flying out onto the field.

Magerkurth tried to avoid Durocher, but Leo kept getting into his way and bumping him, until "the Maje" turned his back and walked down the left-field line. Durocher was trying to step on his feet to trip him when Magerkurth wheeled and threw him out of the game. But in so doing he splattered tobacco juice across Leo's face. So Durocher leaped up at him and spit right in *his* face.

"That'll cost you two hundred fifty dollars and ten days!" Magerkurth roared.

"For what?"

"You spat in my face."

"What the hell do you think this is?" Durocher said, pointing at his own face.

"Mi-i-ine was an accident."

"Not mi-i-ine," replied Leo, mimicking the ump, "mi-i-ine was intentional!"

For telling the truth, Magerkurth said he would forget about the fine and suspension if Leo quickly left the premises. Durocher agreed, but couldn't resist kicking a little dirt on him as he was leaving, and he got fined fifty dollars for that.

Spitting or kicking dirt on the umpire is a time-honored tradition in the managing profession. Tommy Lasorda, for one, always puts a chew in his mouth before going out for an argument. If things get ugly, Lasorda gets real close to the ump and lets some of the tobacco juice accidentally spray him. And the rude tradition of kicking dirt on the umps was carried on by Billy Martin, who thought it was a good way of getting at the umpire without bumping or pushing him; those transgressions can lead to a suspension. You're not allowed to touch the ump during an argument, even with the bill of your cap, so Earl Weaver used to turn his cap around backwards when he was set to argue so he could get right in the umpire's face.

Sticks and stones are verboten when challenging an umpire, but if words are the manager's last resort, he tries to make them good ones. Dick Williams was known for his scathing sarcasm, which he put on display one night when he had enough of Ron Luciano. In the middle of an argument, Williams paused to let Luciano listen to the sound of an entire stadium booing him. "Hear that?" he said. "They're not just booing the call you made. They're booing your entire career!"

Earl Weaver was the most frequently ejected manager of his generation, with ninety-one career dismissals and four suspensions to his credit. To say the least, he was not a favorite with the umpires. Jim Evans referred to Weaver as "the Son of Sam of baseball." To Nick Bremigan, Weaver was "the Ayatollah." And to Rich Garcia, Weaver was simply "a disgrace to the game." Marty Springstead just didn't like his attitude. "That midget can barely see over the top of the dugout steps, and he claims he can see the pitches. He blames every loss on the players, umpires, or ground conditions. He's five hundred and zero in his little mind."

Weaver gave Luciano the impression that he wanted every close call—"He wants you to cheat for him. He wants an unfair advantage." Weaver and Luciano had so many serious rhubarbs that the league office finally took Luciano's umpiring crew off any series involving the Orioles.

Once the umpires formed their own association and had some protection, they were no longer whipping boys, and started to more frequently bump back the managers and talk back as well. A classic manager-umpire argument got a little personal in 1980 in Memorial Stadium when umpire Bill Haller called a balk and Weaver disagreed, to put it mildly. Again, this comes from an on-field mike.

WEAVER Assh, shit!
HALLER: Fuck yourself.

WEAVER: You're here and this crew is here just to fuck us!
[Haller throws him out at this point.]
WEAVER: You couldn't wait to get me out.
HALLER: Earl, you run yourself.
WEAVER: Get your finger off me.
HALLER: You hit me?
WEAVER: Yeah, because you put your finger on me. You do it again
and I'll knock you right on your nose.
HALLER: I didn't touch you. You're lying.
WEAVER: You ain't no good.
HALLER: Nah, you ain't either.
WEAVER: What are you doing here now?
HALLER: Well, why don't you call the league office and tell them.
WEAVER: Don't you think I won't. One day I'll be in the Hall of
Fame, and where will you be?
[Weaver had his last word, and started walking defiantly off the field,
but Haller had a zinger left for him.]
HALLER: Hall of Fame? What for? For fucking up the World Series?
[Referring to Weaver having a 3–1 lead in games against the Pirates
in 1979 and losing.]

There used to be an automatic suspension for saying a certain bad
word, but that rule was thrown out years ago. There is no magic word
that will get you run. It's a matter of different strokes for different
folks. If a manager or a player uses profanity as part of his normal
vocabulary, like Len Dykstra, he is not going to be thrown out for
using it in the heat of an argument. Umpire Eric Gregg put it this
way: "An umpire doesn't eject a manager or player. They eject
themselves. They know exactly what they can say and who they can
say it to. So when somebody is thrown out, he has either completely
lost control, or he intended to be run."

Most umpires do have one word or expression that activates their
sensitive button. One major league umpire has a hairpiece, and anyone who mentions it is finished for that game. Eric Gregg has a weight
problem, and players who want to stick around can't say "Hey-Hey-
Hey!" as if addressing Bill Cosby's Fat Albert character. The legendary large-lipped umpire Bill Klem bore a resemblance to a catfish,

but if you mentioned his nickname, you were gone. In the 1940s umpire Frank Dascoli once had a girl in his room and unfortunately left the shades up. For years afterward, anybody could get excused from the day's game by simply saying, "Hey, Frank, why don't you keep the bleepin' shades down?"

The smart manager learns how to be diplomatic with an umpire. Some have absolutely perfected the game of running out onto the field, riling up the fans, and lighting a fire under their ball club, all without overstepping their bounds. One day in Dodger Stadium the home team was losing 4–0, and Tommy Lasorda ran out to argue a called strike with home-plate umpire Gregg.

When he got to home plate, he said, "Hey Eric, that must have been some pitch." Gregg just smiled. "Yeah, Tommy, he's gotta swing at that pitch." Now Lasorda spread his arms out and waved them. "What am I gonna do? I know he should swing at that pitch and I've told him that." By now the crowd was warming to what they believed to be a rousing argument, and Lasorda started shaking his head in disgust as a whole stadium full of people rose to their feet, urging the manager on to tell off the umpire. Making small talk, Lasorda got the crowd into the game while avoiding arguing about a ball or strike call, which is strictly forbidden.

In the wake of Roger Clemens's quick ejection by home-plate umpire Terry Cooney in game four of the 1990 playoffs, some of today's managers complained that umpires have become too belligerent, temperamental, and confrontational. In the case of Clemens's ejection, lip-readers maintain that he did mouth obscenities at Cooney, but the umpire never took off his mask or left the area of the plate to issue a warning. There was never a chance for Red Sox manager Joe Morgan to intervene and cool things down.

National League umpire Bruce Froemming insists that the new perception of umpires as thin-skinned and overly aggressive is strictly because of today's television exposure: "The guys we think of as the dynamite umpires of the past, guys like Al Barlick, Frank Dascoli, Augie Donatelli, and Shag Crawford, were always in wars, but no one saw it besides the people in the stadium because there was no one to show it. Now we're part of your living room."

One National League manager, who requested anonymity, said he was baited and challenged by umpires when he tried to argue. "They turn on you now," he said, "for no reason at all." American League managers have voiced the same complaints. In May 1990, Seattle manager Jim Lefebvre was ejected by home-plate umpire Dale Ford for yelling the common phrase "Bear down!" In a similar reversal of tradition, umpire Drew Coble ran to the Orioles dugout to admonish manager Frank Robinson after Robinson merely signaled with his hand that a called strike was high.

Managers and umpires are going through a transitional period now. Nobody seems to know just where the line is drawn when it comes to disagreeing with a call. That was never a problem when Bill Klem was the arbiter. He used to signal this point in an argument by literally drawing a line with his foot—cross it and you're gone. Onetime manager Frankie Frisch tried to run around the line, but Klem informed him that he was still out of the game. "The line," Klem bellowed, "extends to infinity!"

Managing the Media

If there's anything baseball beat writers hate, it's a manager who won't write their stories for them. When Walter Alston took over the Dodgers in 1954, he had two stock phrases he used with the writers. One was "I'll have to wait and see"; the other was "It would be silly to discuss things I don't know anything about yet."

While the colorful Casey Stengel became a favorite of sportswriters, he wasn't always so adept with the media. At Stengel's first press conference in New York, after taking over the Yankees in 1949, he was uncharacteristically nervous and edgy. He referred to Yankee president Dan Topping as "Bob" (Topping's playboy brother). Then one of the writers asked about managing DiMaggio, and Stengel said he didn't know DiMaggio. What he meant was that he had played and managed in the National League and only knew the great DiMag by reputation. But it did sound odd.

Of course, Stengel later won the press over with his insights, storytelling, and sense of humor, not to mention his style of delivery. And he used the press to great advantage, as a way of sending his players a message. He once told a reporter that Whitey Ford didn't always tip off his infielders that he was going to throw an off-speed pitch. Stengel wanted Ford to get a strong message in the press instead of just a hint from the manager. Whitey Herzog said, "Casey was the best public relations man who ever lived. He knew exactly what he was doing all the time."

How the manager deals with the media today is one of the most important parts of the job. "We're more of a media society now," former Royals and current Braves GM John Schuerholz told Jon Boswell, "and the manager is the one who presents your organization to the public. We're the number-one fishbowl industry in the country. The manager has a huge responsibility as a spokesman. Some old-style managers haven't been able to withstand the crunch of that. It's no accident that the most successful managers—Herzog, Weaver, Lasorda, Anderson—often speak to the team by what they say on TV and in the papers. You don't need team meetings to set your club's tone."

Of course, what appears in the press is not always the result of a manager's well-laid master plan, as when Billy Martin said about Steinbrenner and Reggie Jackson: "They deserve each other. One's a born liar and the other's convicted." The two sportswriters who were present when Martin made the famous 1978 comment after having a few drinks in an airport bar were Murray Chass of *The New York Times* and Henry Hecht of the *New York Post*. For a week Martin denied that he had said it, but eventually he had to admit the slur that hastened his firing. Up to that point, Hecht had an uneventful relationship with Martin, but from then on the writer became his nemesis.

During the Reggie/Billy wars, Hecht had taken the side of Jackson, writing that Martin had tried to drive his star crazy, pull a *Gaslight* on him, with the manager in the role of Charles Boyer and Jackson the Ingrid Bergman figure. Hecht was also the first sportswriter to characterize Martin in print as a paranoid alcoholic.

The tension between the two came to a head when Martin returned to manage the Yankees once again. In May 1983, the team wasn't playing well, and Steinbrenner called a team meeting to give the players a little pep talk. Then Martin held his own meeting, and told the team not to listen to George because he didn't know what the hell he was talking about. The beat writers found out about the meeting on the condition that they couldn't write about it. Hecht heard about it by accident from a Yankee player's agent, and wrote the story.

The next time Hecht came to the ballpark, Martin called a team meeting for everybody to attend—writers, broadcasters, hangers-on—with the express purpose of ripping Hecht in public. "Don't talk to Henry Hecht," Martin railed. "There he is, and if there was ever a fuckin' bastard, there he is. He's the worst fuckin' scrounge ever to come around this clubhouse. He doesn't care if he hurts you or gets you fired, he just wants to use you. He got me fired twice, and now he's trying to make it a third time. And if you talk to him, don't talk to me, 'cause I don't want to have anything to do with anyone who talks to this little prick."

"You're paranoid," said Hecht.

"I'm not paranoid. I don't have to be paranoid to see that you're a little prick. You're not welcome in my office. You can come into the clubhouse—I wouldn't ever take away a man's right to earn a living—but you're not welcome in my office because I don't trust a fuckin' thing you say."

"You can imagine what I think of you."

"I read about it in the papers every day, you asshole. I don't need to imagine it. You're not welcome in my office. If that little bastard comes in here, I'll put him in the fuckin' whirlpool."

Some of the Yankees—Don Baylor, Dave Winfield, and Ken Griffey, among others—were conspicuous in ignoring Martin's edict and immediately talked with Hecht. To Hecht, it was the second time that Martin had tried to sabotage his career. "I have a very long memory," he said. "Martin died owing me two apologies. I pitied the man in some ways because he was such a brutally unhappy character. He had great baseball instincts until alcohol rotted out his brain in the late '70s and early '80s."

Steinbrenner came close to firing Martin at this time, but nothing had given the Boss what he considered "just cause." Instead he humiliated and infuriated Martin by firing his pitching coach and drinking buddy Art Fowler. At that point Martin, upset and frustrated, did a stunningly stupid thing. He saw an attractive young woman in the clubhouse, chatting with his players. Assuming that she was someone's guest, he ordered her from the room. She was Deborah Henschel, a reporter from *The New York Times*. Henschel left the clubhouse and went to the visitors' clubhouse. There one of the stadium security guards challenged her credentials and wouldn't let her in. She figured that Martin had called ahead to keep her out, and so she telephoned her desk for instructions. The deputy sports editor called the Yankees and spoke to Steinbrenner, and the incident was reconstructed.

Martin, it was alleged, said rough things to the woman from the *Times*. It was the excuse Steinbrenner needed to fire Martin once again.

A manager has to take what the media dishes out, even when they're circling around you like vultures. With the cloud of the Pete Rose investigation hanging over the Reds in 1989, reporters swamped the team, following the troubled manager. Still, the Reds got off fast and were in first place in April and May. Then injuries hit some of the major players, and they faded badly. So a lot of sportswriters fell over each other writing that Rose's problems, not the injuries, were crippling the team.

Managerial exasperation reached its zenith when the Chicago Cubs got off to a woeful 5–14 start in April 1983. A manager can sense when the wolves are at the door barking for his job, and manager Lee Elia, in this famous monologue, let it all hang out for the stunned reporters in his office. The language of defeat in baseball is generally X-rated, and so the text is presented here, from a bootleg recording, expurgated somewhat. Of the peaks of baseball-induced frustration on record, this is the high Himalayas:

"Let's talk about the great support the players are supposed to get around here. I haven't seen it this year. Don't ask me about any specific play, I won't answer it. I won't talk about specific plays. The name of the game is hit the ball, catch the ball, and get the job done. Every time we lose a close game it's magnified why this guy bunted and why this guy popped up, or that guy threw a wild pitch. That's baseball, fellas, that's baseball, that's how the runs are scored, that's how the balance goes cockeyed. That's the difference between victory and defeat. All right, they don't show because we're five and fourteen. And unfortunately that's the criterion of the dumb 15 percent that come out to day baseball, and the other 85 percent are out earning a living.

"I'll tell you, it'll take more than a five and thirteen or five and fourteen to destroy the makeup of this club. I guarantee you that.

There's some pros out there who want to play this game. It's a disheartening situation we're in right now. Anybody who was associated with the Cub organization four or five years ago, they come back and see the multitude of progress that's been made, then five–fourteen doesn't negate all that work. Ya got 143 games left. What I'm trying to say is, don't rip them guys out there. You want to rip somebody, rip my ass! But don't rip them guys, because they're giving everything they can give, and right now they're trying to do more than God gave them, and that's why we make the simple mistakes, that's exactly why."

A Decade of Big-Game Managing Blunders

Everyday managing is tough enough on the manager's central nervous system. But big-game managing is something else entirely. These are the ones that decide a pennant at the end of the regular season, or the key playoff and World Series games. And the effect on managers ought to be clinically studied.

The big games that a manager remembers the longest are the losses for which he feels partly responsible, when he made a decision based on what he felt was his best chance to win, and it didn't work out. Nobody dissects the blunders of the victors. But when it blows up in your face, and a chance to win a championship slips away, managers generally have to face the music.

Some managers prefer not to take the rap for their calls. After Bobby Thomson homered off Ralph Branca in the 1951 National League playoff, Brooklyn manager Charley Dressen blamed the pitching coach, Clyde Sukeforth, for selecting the wrong pitcher to come into the game. Was there a sign on Dressen's desk reading "The buck stops with the pitching coach"? For telling Dressen over the bullpen phone that Erskine was bouncing his curveball, leading to the insertion of Branca, Sukeforth wound up with a knife hanging out of his back. He was fired, and Dressen kept his job.

The Yankees were not quite as understanding when Casey Stengel lost the seventh game of the 1960 World Series. Stengel went through the tortuous twists and turns of this game using pitchers who were tired and hurt, and had Ralph Terry warming up three different times in the bullpen. When Terry finally did come into the game to get the last out in the eighth inning, he may have already left his best stuff in the bullpen. The first man he faced in the ninth was Bill Mazeroski, who homered on the second pitch to win the Series.

Stengel had wanted to win another championship to change the minds of the Yankee brain trust. They felt it was time for him to step down but it was the Mazeroski home run that did indeed end Stengel's career.

Here is one observer's choice of

THE WORST MANAGING MISTAKES OF THE LAST TEN YEARS

1981 World Series, Los Angeles Dodgers vs. New York Yankees

The Yankees found themselves down to the Dodgers 3–2 in games, but the Series was moving back to Yankee Stadium. The game was tied at 1–1 in the fifth inning, when the Yankees loaded the bases with two outs. Manager Bob Lemon summoned his best pinch-hitter, Bobby Murcer, to hit for the starter, Tommy John.

At the time Lemon made the move, John didn't appear angry so much as stunned, and he could be seen laughing and talking to himself in the corner of the dugout. John hadn't been touched by the Dodgers yet in the Series, and was definitely on his game this night. Murcer flied out to deep right field, and the threat was over.

It was a move that Lemon never would have made in a regular season game, but he figured that he had to do something to win in a game this big. Years later, John conceded that a manager might make such a move, but insisted that if you do pinch-hit in a must game, "You have to come in with your best pitcher, you have to come in with Gossage, your stopper. But George Frazier?"

Lemon put in his middle-inning pitcher in a situation that didn't call for a middle-reliever at all. Frazier got hit, and was charged with his record third loss of the Series, as the season ended for the Yankees. Did Lemon panic by taking out an effective starter so early and thereby blow the Series?

We trust that Bob Lemon hasn't lost too much sleep over this game. In his Hall of Fame acceptance speech, Lem said that he never took a game home with him. "I left it in a bar somewhere along the way," he confided.

1982 ALCS, California Angels vs. Milwaukee Brewers

Gene Mauch has frequently been heralded as the smartest tactical manager in the game, a baseball genius who didn't get to the World Series because of bad breaks, or because he just didn't have the horses. If that is the case, he has been most unlucky, but in a few instances he brought his own black cloud with him.

His 1964 Phillies did a famous El Foldo when they blew a six-and-one-half-game lead by losing their last ten games of the season, losing the pennant to the Cards on the final day of the season. In that pennant stretch, Mauch repeatedly pitched his two best starters, Jim Bunning and Chris Short, on two days' rest, five times each, and lost and lost and lost.

In 1982, by using the same strategy, he became the first manager to blow a 2–0 lead in the best-of-five playoffs. The California Angels won the first two games over the Brewers before the series shifted to Milwaukee. After the Brewers won the third game, Mauch tabbed the thirty-nine-year-old Tommy John to pitch on three days' rest instead of his usual four. (Didn't any managers know how to use this guy in the postseason?) John had nothing, threw three wild pitches, got bombed, and the Brewers won 9–5. The Brewers then had all the momentum, and won their third straight at home the following day.

Before the World Series was over, Mauch was fired, left to lie back on his bed of nails to contemplate more abstract tactical maneuvers, or maybe just how he crashed and burned again in Old Milwaukee. "If it's true you learn from adversity," he once said, "then I must be the smartest sumbitch in the whole world."

1983 World Series, Philadelphia Phillies vs. Baltimore Orioles

Three aging ex-Reds—Pete Rose, Joe Morgan, and Tony Perez, sometimes referred to as the Wheeze Kids—were members of a Phillies team that went 26–5 down the stretch to win the National League East under manager Paul Owens. But only Morgan was playing regularly by the end of the regular season. When postseason play began, Rose was back in the starting lineup because Len Matuszek, who had been recalled from the minors in September, was ineligible.

The Phillies beat the Dodgers in the playoffs, then split the first two World Series games in Baltimore. Returning to Philadelphia for that third game, manager Owens made a move he knew wasn't going to be easy—he benched Pete Rose. Wasn't this the reason the Phillies had made Rose baseball's first $2 million-per-year player, to perform in showcase games like this and provide his leadership and Series experience? Owens didn't think so. The Baltimore pitcher was left-hander Mike Flanagan, and Tony Perez was going to play first base.

The trouble wasn't benching Rose; managers get paid for making unpopular decisions in the crunch. The trouble was that Owens, not so affectionately nicknamed "The Pope," did it as an imperial decree, without consulting Rose or even telling him that he wasn't going to start. This humiliated and rankled Rose, who burst past the assembled sportswriters before the game and told Howard Cosell and an audience of 70 million on ABC that he was embarrassed, apparently unaware that he was also insulting teammate and friend Tony Perez. Rose was becoming a free agent again after the Series, and his own motives were nakedly clear. He was auditioning for the other twenty-five teams so he could play another two years and smash Ty Cobb's hit record.

So Perez played in Game Three and got a base hit, but the Phillies lost, 3–2. Owens inserted Rose into the lineup for the rest of the Series against both righties and lefties, and he wound up with as many hits in the Series as any player. But the damage had already been done, and Philadelphia also lost games Four and Five.

The hubbub about the decision moved the focus from the games at hand to the problems within the Phillies clubhouse. Owens was exposed in the debacle as a manager who was not willing or able to communicate with or control his ball club when they were only three wins from a world title.

1984 World Series, Detroit Tigers vs. San Diego Padres

Ahead 3–1 in games, the Tigers were only one victory from becoming world champs. But if they lost the fifth game at home, the Series would return to San Diego. The pivotal moment of Game Five came in the bottom of the eighth inning, with the Tigers up 5–4, and runners on second and third. The hitter was Kirk Gibson, and the pitcher was Goose Gossage. Gibson had already homered in the first inning, so manager Dick Williams went out to the mound to instruct Gossage that he wanted an intentional pass. That way Gossage could face the right-handed Lance Parrish with the bases loaded, and try to get out of the inning with a double-play grounder.

But Gossage told Williams he wanted to pitch to Gibson, and Williams, normally not given to second-guessing himself, started to waver. This wasn't the same dominant Gossage who posted a 0.77 ERA during the strike-shortened 1981 season. He was still a power pitcher, but one who didn't strike a great deal of fear into left-handed sluggers. In fact, in the Tiger dugout, manager Sparky Anderson was telling Gibson that Gossage would never pitch to him; and Gibson, by way of reply, bet Anderson ten bucks that if he did, Kirk would blast the pitch out of the park.

To the great surprise of the opposing manager, Williams let Gossage talk him into challenging Gibson. Before Williams could get settled back in the dugout, the Goose's fastball was indeed hit deep into the upper deck in right field for a three-run homer that effectively clinched the championship for the Tigers.

1985 NLCS, Los Angeles Dodgers vs. St. Louis Cardinals

The 1985 playoff in the National League between the Cardinals and the Dodgers came down to one crucial at-bat. The Cardinals were losing the sixth game, 5–4, in the ninth inning, and Tom Niedenfuer was trying to nail down the win for the Dodgers. Willie McGee got a one-out single and stole second. Ozzie Smith walked, and then Tom Herr moved them to second and third with a groundball to the right side. The batter was Jack Clark.

Whitey Herzog does not often point out the mistakes of the opposing manager, because nothing is as true in baseball as the adage about how what goes around comes around, but in this case, Herzog couldn't resist giving Lasorda the rip job.

To Herzog, Jack Clark hitting with two out and a base open is "the ideal place for an intentional walk." Lasorda elected to have Niedenfuer pitch to Clark instead of loading the bases, which Herzog called "a mistake." "If Tommy walks Clark and brings in a lefty to pitch to Van Slyke, I would have countered with Brian Harper, the only right-handed pinch-hitter I had left. I would rather let Brian Harper try to beat me than Jack Clark, but what the hell? A manager has to go with what's in his gut, and we've all been wrong now and again. Tommy told Niedenfuer to pitch to Clark."

Niedenfuer had struck out Clark just a few innings previously, so Lasorda went with the hot hand. But Herzog thought of Clark as "the best clutch fastball hitter in baseball." Some managers just don't want to load the bases, since it puts pressure on the pitcher, and pits one hitter's on-base average against another hitter's batting average. Clark ended the calculations by hitting the first pitch high into the left-field pavilion for a three-run homer, and pointed into the Dodger dugout at Lasorda as he circled the bases.

1986 ALCS, California Angels vs. Boston Red Sox

No team had come from three runs down in their last at-bat to win a playoff or World Series game. In the space of five days in the fall of '86, it happened three times. There were a lot of blown leads and exciting finishes, the kind of games that can make at least one of the managers look pretty bad.

In the playoff with the Red Sox, Gene Mauch, now back managing the Angels again, got as close as you can get to the World Series and still wind up chain-smoking and watching it on television. In Game Five at Anaheim Stadium, Mauch went into the ninth inning with a three-run lead. Starter Mike Witt gave up a single to Bull Buckner, fanned Jim Rice, and then threw a curveball on the outside corner to Don Baylor, a very good down-breaking pitch, and Baylor incredibly took the ball over the wall in left, just going down to get the pitch and muscling it with his tremendous strength.

Witt hadn't lost it yet. He was the best right-hander the Angels had, and he recovered by popping up Evans, so he wasn't done for the day. The next batter after Baylor was Rich Gedman. The Angels still led 5–4. Gedman, however, was three for three, and Mauch made the move to his bullpen to bring in lefty Gary Lucas, and Lucas hit Gedman on the hip. Mauch went to the pen again with Dave Henderson at the plate, and Donnie Moore came in to face him. Moore hung a breaking pitch and Henderson hit a two-run homer to give Boston the lead.

Mauch wound up managing the inning by being afraid of the wrong guy, and that's how you end up pacing the floors at three in the morning, afraid to look in the mirror because, as Lefty Frizzell sang, "It tears me up to see a grown man cry."

The Angels tied that game in the bottom of the ninth, which turned out to merely prolong the agony. Mauch left a shell-shocked Donnie Moore in the game and got beat on an eleventh-inning sacrifice fly to center off the bat of, naturally, the gap-toothed menace, Dave Henderson.

1986 World Series, New York Mets vs. Boston Red Sox

There were two outs and nobody on base. The Red Sox were closing in on their first world title since 1919. Calvin Schiraldi was on the mound for the Sox. He'd been a strong closer for them in the latter half of the '86 season, but had faltered of late. Now he retired Wally Backman on a fly to left and Keith Hernandez on a deep fly to center. Gary Carter stood at the plate with a 2–1 count. The Red Sox led by two runs, so Schiraldi threw the fastball, coming right down the pipe, and Carter singled sharply to left.

Kevin Mitchell hit a hanging curveball into center field, one of the few curveballs he hit safely the whole season. Then came an excruciating at-bat by Ray Knight. He fought off several pitches with two strikes, got jammed again, but finally nudged the ball off the handle of the bat, a dying quail just over the infielders' heads into center field. Carter scored and the Mets trailed by a run. Manager John

McNamara replaced Schiraldi, who by this time looked white as Caspar, with Bob Stanley.

The move was an eerie reflection of the Donnie Moore appearance of just ten days earlier, a formerly successful stopper who had fallen on hard times, now routinely booed by hometown fans, and, suddenly, with everything on the line, getting a last-ditch chance to totally redeem his position in the team's history.

Mookie Wilson stepped up to the plate, one of the few Mets remaining from the awful New York teams of the early '80s. Mookie hung tough in one of the great all-time pressure at-bats, fouling off tough sinking pitches from Stanley until, with the count 2–2, Wilson jackknifed away from one of the nastier sinkers. The ball got by catcher Gedman for a wild pitch, and Mitchell came in from third to tie the game.

The fans were up screaming, the Red Sox players had their hearts in their mouths, and John McNamara didn't come out of the dugout. Just let 'em play, act as if it never happened, as if professionals don't get stunned like normal people. So Stanley was left alone on the mound with his thoughts as if he were leprous, and still had to continue his battle with Mookie Wilson, this time with the winning run on second base.

After fouling off two more pitches, Wilson hit a little topspin grounder to first baseman Bill Buckner. It would be a very close play at first base, as Wilson was beating Stanley to the bag, and Buckner was crouched on damaged legs. The ball stayed down under his glove and slowly rolled into right field. That was the ballgame. The first words out of Met announcer Gary Thorne's mouth were, "What is Bill Buckner doing on the field?"

What Bill Buckner was doing was getting Bob Stanley and Rich Gedman off the hook as the all-time Series goat, and winning the horns for himself. Buckner was customarily taken out of games in which the Red Sox led late, usually replaced by the much more mobile Dave Stapleton. McNamara had made this move in seven consecutive postseason games, most often after lifting Buckner for a pinch-runner. McNamara actually had an opportunity to pinch-run for him in the Red Sox half of the tenth inning when Buckner was hit by a pitch. But he left him in.

While Buckner had been a decent-fielding first baseman in his career, it is always better to have someone out there who can run, and Buckner had shown several times in the Series that he really couldn't.

How bad were Buckner's pins? One ankle was already kaput, bone grinding against bone, and he had surgery on it only a few days after the Series was over. Buckner had injured the other foot in the playoffs, tearing his Achilles' tendon, and it was a wonder he could play at all. For hours before each game he iced his feet, one of his knees, his quadriceps and hamstrings; he took cortisone shots and anti-inflammatory pills.

"He has good hands," McNamara said after the game. "He was moving pretty well tonight." Leaving Buckner on the field, presumably for sentimental reasons, was what ultimately cost McNamara. This criticism assumes that sentiment should never enter into game-level decisions at the pinnacle of baseball. Or should it? "The only question," said Buckner, "is whether McNamara should have gotten me out of that game at the time." The only question for the Red Sox front office was when they were going to fire McNamara, which they did a few months into the 1987 season.

1987 World Series, St. Louis Cardinals vs. Minnesota Twins

Who has the heart to criticize Whitey Herzog for taking out Joe Magrane in the fifth inning of the seventh game of the World Series, and bringing in Danny Cox, who got thoroughly lambasted? Herzog had shown a lot of faith in Magrane, making him the youngest pitcher to start the first and seventh games of a Series. He just figured that pitching under that kind of draining pressure, with the Metrodome noise of a supersonic jet taking off in his ears, was enough for a rookie. Plus a runner was just called safe at first on what should have been a 3–1 putout, and that kind of adversity is always a danger sign for all but the most veteran pitchers. Herzog thought it was time for a pitching change.

Managers are usually criticized for letting a pitcher stay in too long, maybe just one batter too long, enough to lose the ballgame. But in this case, many of the Cardinals wondered later what would have happened if the change *hadn't* been made. Magrane was throwing nasty stuff at the end of the '87 season, and he wasn't getting hit in Game Seven either. He had in fact truly arrived, and the following year would win the NL ERA title. But enough speculation. Herzog, the boss, preferred the veteran but oft-injured Cox, who had already lost the fifth game.

Cox came in with the Cardinals leading 2–1. His location was poor, and his strikes were straight as a string. He allowed the Twins to tie the game in the fifth and go ahead in the sixth, and Frank Viola and Ken Reardon held the lead for Minnesota.

1988 NLCS, New York Mets vs. Los Angeles Dodgers

When the New York Mets faced the Los Angeles Dodgers in the 1988 playoffs, it figured to be something of a mismatch, even if the Dodgers had played very well down the stretch, featuring Orel Hershiser's record scoreless-inning string. The Minnesota Twins had shown, as other teams had, that you can win a world championship with two good pitchers (Blyleven and Viola), especially if you have a good bullpen stopper like Jeff Reardon. But even with Hershiser so unhittable, the Mets had beaten the Dodgers silly all year long.

The Mets led the series, two games to one, when they started Dwight Gooden at Shea Stadium. Gooden carried a two-run lead into the ninth. With one out, he got John Shelby down to 0–2, and then wound up walking him by displaying one of the sure signs of the tired pitcher—getting wild high.

The next hitter, Mike Scioscia, wound up guessing right on a high-velocity fastball that he could nonetheless handle, and drove it over the fence for a stunning, game-tying homer. The Mets eventually would lose the game on a twelfth-inning home run by Kirk Gibson off Roger McDowell.

Manager Davey Johnson drew some criticism for not bringing in his recently dominant lefty Randy Myers in such a big game, the chance to go up 3–1 in the series. The reason he didn't lift a finger in the ninth probably had something to do with the fact that Gooden had never won a postseason game in his already glorious career. He had lost 1–0 to Mike Scott in game one of the '86 playoff, then in game five dueled Nolan Ryan to a 1–1 tie in a game won by the Mets in extra innings. In the '86 World Series, he lost twice. Earlier in the Dodger series he had pitched well against Hershiser in game one and not gotten the decision, so Johnson understandably wanted to see his ace get over the hump by going all the way. He didn't want to tamper with Gooden's confidence by even warming somebody up. It's your game, he was saying, I have total confidence that you'll get through the ninth.

1989 NLCS, Chicago Cubs vs. San Francisco Giants

It was, let's face it, the Year of the Zim. Students of Zimmerology are well aware that throughout the years, many of his strategic moves have been traced to the steel plate he has in his head from a beaning—but it doesn't matter how many refrigerator magnets you can stick on his noggin, he was still 1989's Manager of the Year.

It was the season in which Don Zimmer shed the big monkey off his back from the Red Sox years. The monkey from 1978 was actually more like a gorilla, as Boston blew one of the biggest leads in major league history, finally losing in a playoff to a team of hardened money players on the Yankees. Zimmer's Sox had players like Fred Lynn, Carl Yastrzemski, Jim Rice, Carlton Fisk, Rick Burleson, Dwight Evans, Butch Hobson, and George Scott. They hit homers at a record clip at several points during the year. But as usual they were thin in the pitching department, although it didn't help that Zimmer pitched undistinguished minor leaguers like Bobby Sprowl against the Yankees rather than the Spaceman, Bill Lee, who had dubbed his manager "the designated gerbil."

But even managers accused of blowing a pennant with a talented team get other chances to manage, especially when their grade-school hometown friend, Jim Frey, is the general manager of a major league ball club. Frey brought Zimmer to Chicago, and at first the team struggled. They won seventy-seven games in 1988 while blowing the incredible total of twenty-seven save opportunities out of the bullpen. So once they got Mitch Williams to anchor the bullpen as their stopper, they figured to be better than a .500 team, and maybe improve on that.

The maybes that worked out for the Cubs were many, such as the emergence of rookie center fielder Jerome Walton, who was a defensive whiz from the start, but also showed he could hit major league pitching. Then an injury to left-fielder Mitch Webster forced Zimmer to play Dwight Smith in left field, and Smith wound up hitting .324. On the pitching staff, rookie phenom Mike Harkey didn't come through, but former phenom Mike Bielecki did, and the Cubs were in the race all the way.

Zimmer kept things interesting in his inimitable fashion, frequently utilizing bizarre strategy. One of his favorite moves was to send the runners with the bases loaded and one out when the count got to 3–2. As long as the hitter didn't strike out, it was a good play, and it sure put pressure on the pitcher to have all the runners going.

Zimmer's Cubs played with enthusiasm and were a pleasure to watch. And then Ryne Sandberg got homer-crazy in midsummer and all the other contenders in the NL East began to fade. The Cubs wound up winning the division fairly easily, giving Zimmer a chance to demonstrate his wily ways in the National League Championship Series.

In game one against the San Francisco Giants, Zimmer started his young ace, Greg Maddux, who could not pinpoint his pitches in the early going. He was spitting nonstop in an embarrassing display of nerves, and had nothing. Maddux gave up a homer to Will Clark, but the game was still close when Clark came up again in the fourth inning, this time with the bases loaded.

Zimmer waddled out to the mound and everybody expected he would take Maddux out. Instead he left him in, and the first pitch to Clark was a room-service meatball right down the pipe, and Clark, eyes popping out of his head, whacked it over the right-field bleachers, onto Sheffield Avenue, for a grand slam.

In Zimmer's defense, he didn't tell Maddux to throw the ball right down the middle, nor did he throw the pitch, but perhaps some of those runs and the first-game loss should be charged to Zim. The Cubs managed to win only one game before being eliminated by the

Giants. Zimmer responded to questions about his playoff performance in typically candid fashion: "We didn't pitch good. We didn't
hit good. Every move I made turned to garbage. Most of the moves
I made during the season were on the plus side. I didn't manage any
differently during the playoffs. I did what I wanted to do, just like
all year. It just turned to dirt. Everything I did stunk."

PART 3

CLUBHOUSE

CHEMISTRY

"Dissension Does It Again"

On the simplest level, baseball games are decided by who scores the most runs on a given day. But what about the interpersonal dynamics, what Graham Greene called "the human factor"? In a six-month, 162-game baseball season (or longer, if the team is good, and lucky), ballplayers live together as a kind of surrogate family. "Team chemistry" is the buzzword used to describe this complex of factors—the interplay between players, between manager and players, players and press, even players and fans. The better the team chemistry, the better a team's chances, usually. But how to get cooking? That is the question, dear reader. Good chemistry remains one of the game's true intangibles. While many acknowledge its importance, few are bold enough to proclaim that they know how to cultivate it or maintain it once they've got it.

There are no statistics for how veteran leadership enables a team to weather a string of tough losses, or helps a team get over the hump when they hit a stretch of draining extra-inning games or hot-weather doubleheaders during the dog days of July and August. Just what was Don Baylor's value in the clubhouse of the '86 pennant-winning Red Sox or the '87 championship Twins?

In some cases, a team is said to have talent, but still has to "learn how to win." When the Pittsburgh Pirates commanded first place in the summer of 1990, manager Jim Leyland wondered himself about how far the team's psychological makeup was taking them. "I keep hearing about all this so-called continuity we've got with the players here, and how much they've been through together. I heard about the leadership Wally Backman has brought to our clubhouse. And we do have continuity. We have been through a lot. Wally is a hell of a little leader. But you know why we are where we are right now? Bobby Bonilla, Barry Bonds, Andy Van Slyke, Jose Lind. Those are talented people. Togetherness is terrific, but give me talent anytime."

Leyland's point is an interesting one. Does good team chemistry really translate into heads-up, hustling, clutch play, or is it winning itself that produces the good chemistry? When the Pittsburgh Pirates won in 1979, led by father figure Willie "Pops" Stargell, their theme song was "We Are Fam-a-lee." Many of the players treated their success as if the good feeling in the clubhouse was responsible for their winning the World Series, although a few Pirates credited the Lord Almighty. There was another possibility. A lot of Pirate players were having banner years—Dave Parker, Willie Stargell, Bill Robinson, Phil Garner, right on down the line. Leadoff man Omar Moreno, for instance, later known as "Omar the Outmaker," hit .282, stole seventy-seven bases, and drove in sixty-nine runs!

The fact is, these magic moments of brotherhood are will-'o-the-wisp in baseball. A few years after the Pirates won it all, the only good feelings in the Pirate clubhouse seemed to be supported by generous amounts of nose candy. As for the 1990 Pirate team, they won the Eastern Division despite strains within the family. And the strains got worse in their hard-fought playoff series with the Cincinnati Reds. With their MVP, Barry Bonds, failing to hit, the pressure on him increased so much that he publicly lashed out at a teammate. That was Jeff King, who asked Leyland to take him out of a game because his back was hurting him to the point where he had difficulty bending over for ground balls.

After the season, the Pirates management worried about how they could afford signing their impending free agents, including Bonds, to multi-year contracts. Bonds took the Pirates to arbitration for his 1991 salary and lost for the second year in a row; he would receive $2.3 million instead of the $3.5 million he wanted. Bonds didn't take losing gracefully, saying that he wouldn't sign with the Pirates when he became a free agent, "even if they gave me $100 million." When he reported to spring training, he sulked. His frustration spilled over one afternoon into shouting matches with a photographer, a coach, and then an obscenity-laced *tête-à-tête* with his manager. "I've been kissing your butt for years!" yelled Leyland. "If you don't want to be here, then get the hell out!" The sporting press made much of the Bucs' brouhaha, and predicted a team collapse. But the team got off to the best start in baseball through the first forty games of the '91 season, indicating how well the key Pirate players were able to separate the off-field turmoil from their professional performance.

Tommy Lasorda is among those who think that chemistry is overrated. Two weeks after Kirk Gibson was reported to have requested a trade from the Dodgers in 1990, he could be heard screaming from behind the closed door of manager Lasorda's office. Gibby was distressed at being switched back and forth in the batting order from second to third, and playing out of position in center field. "I'm not a fucking puppet!" was one of the rants that was clearly audible to his teammates and the press. When Lasorda emerged, he was asked by the media if this tirade could affect the team's chemistry. "Chemistry?" he replied. "What's that? I think I took it in high school."

Everyone knows what bad chemistry is, however; it leaves a smell. When Whitey Herzog left the Cardinals in July 1990, several players commented on how the attitudes and relationships between teammates had become troublesome. Some traced the problems to the fact that there were ten players on the Cards who could become free agents. As pitcher Scott Terry said, "Any reporter, coach, or manager who has spent any time in this locker room knows that there's a chemistry problem. . . . I'd say there's a lot more selfish players in the game who are concerned with themselves and their statistics because that's the basis on which they're paid."

Herzog got tired of seeing players laughing on the bench when the team was throwing games away. On one occasion he walked over to two amused Cardinals after an inning when a botched double play

allowed two runs to score. "What's so damn funny?" Herzog demanded. After ten years in St. Louis he quit because, he said, "I just
couldn't get the players to play."

Looking back, Herzog said, "All of a sudden, team baseball is
gone. Especially for a guy in his walk [free agent] year. He doesn't
want to give himself up and hit the ball to the right side. Oh, he
might act like he's doing it, but it doesn't happen."

Consider what happened to the San Diego Padres, after a strong
1989 finish that left them just three games from first place. In the off-
season, they traded for superstar Joe Carter, and a lot of experts felt
the Padres would win the division title in 1990. But something went
awry. When Mike Pagliarulo came to the Padres from the Yankees,
he immediately remarked that one of his new teammates cared only
about his hits. "If we win and he goes oh for four, he's ticked. If he
gets his hits and we lose, that's fine with him. He doesn't give a bleep
about this team, and that's weak."

Tony Gwynn thought Pags was referring to him, and fired back.
This led to a closed-door, players-only clubhouse meeting in May.
Players let it leak to the press that Jack Clark and Garry Templeton
had blasted Gwynn for caring more about his batting average than
winning. As Clark later explained, "I don't buy his crap of being
upset after games we win, when he doesn't have a good game. He
says he does that because he gets mad at himself. That's bleep. You
win as a team, and you lose as a team."

One of the things the accusations revolved around was Gwynn's
habit of bunting a runner at second base over to third instead of just
trying to hit a ground ball to the right side, "giving himself up," as
they say, to move the runner. Clark and some others saw his bunting
in that situation as a way to protect his precious batting average. But
Gwynn is not really a very good pull hitter, so he considered bunting
to be the best way of getting that runner to third. Out of such mis-
understandings, whole seasons can go up in smoke.

After the All-Star break, as the underachieving Padres fell out of
contention, bad feelings surfaced again. Clark accused some of his
teammates of "just going through the motions." Then in September
Gwynn found a toy figurine of himself hanging by a chain in the

Padres' dugout. Gwynn asked a photographer to take a picture of it, and hung the photo in his locker. A week later Gwynn fractured a finger when he collided with the outfield wall. After he underwent surgery in mid-September, he cleaned out his locker and went home for the season. Gwynn, acknowledged as one of the hardest-working and most complete players in the majors, was just disgusted by it all.

Indeed, there was so much bickering, back-stabbing, and finger-pointing among the players that pitcher Ed Whitson was amazed there wasn't a good old-fashioned fistfight. "I think maybe the only thing that kept that from happening," he said, "is if that occurred, it might have turned into a brawl with all of us knocking the shit out of each other."

Clark said it wasn't just the players who were at each other's throats. "There were a lot of distractions, a lot of in-house fighting. You had coaches against coaches; manager against coaches; general manager against manager; owners against general manager."

Clark got his nickname of "Jack the Ripper" for the hellacious hacks he takes at the plate, but it could just as easily apply to his outspokenness. Even after Clark was signed as a free agent by the Red Sox he continued firing broadsides at Gwynn. "Mr. Padre?" he asked. "Mr. San Diego? Don't make me laugh."

From spring training camp in 1991, Gwynn felt he had to reply: "Let's talk about some of his deficiencies. Let's talk about him walking 104 times, being a number-four hitter. Let's talk about him not flying on team flights. Let's talk about him getting booted out of games on a called strike three. I think anytime he opens his mouth he's telling people just what kind of guy he is." Gwynn got off to a hot start in '91 and stayed that way, leading the league with an average over .350 as the Padres headed toward the All-Star break. Several enthusiastic young players were brought up, and the foul atmosphere in San Diego appeared to have been washed away as if by a stiff sea breeze.

What comes first, the bad chemistry or the losing? The New York Yankees were in the World Series five years in a row, from 1960 to 1964. When the Yankee dynasty suddenly fell apart in 1965, Jim

Bouton recalled the marked change in the atmosphere. "All the good chemistry went out the window. It was an extremely unhappy clubhouse that year, and everybody was in a bad mood. These are very powerful people used to having control of their destinies, controlling all situations, but when you put us all together in a losing situation, it's like taking rats and putting them in a cage where they can't get out and turning up the electricity. You can imagine what they would do to each other. And this is what was happening at the end. You see losing clubs bicker, and you think maybe if they pulled together they would win. No, that's not it. If they won, they would pull together."

Nothing affected team chemistry quite so dramatically as the integration of the first black ballplayer into a big-league clubhouse. That happened in 1947 when Jackie Robinson joined the Brooklyn Dodgers. The path-breaking move was veiled in secrecy by Branch Rickey, who had become general manager of the Dodgers in 1942. He began his experiment with a deception: he said he was bringing a team called the Brooklyn Brown Dodgers into the Negro League and installing them in Ebbets Field where they would play when the big-league team was on the road. This way he had his best scouts looking for the best black players around the country. One of those scouts, Clyde Sukeforth, brought Jackie Robinson to him.

Rickey had a very definite idea about the kind of man he was looking for, because he felt the first black in baseball not only had to be a great player but had to have the strength and intelligence not to react to the provocation he was sure to endure. If there were incidents of retaliation, Rickey feared that integration of the major leagues might be set back twenty years. But he didn't want a gentle soul, either; he wanted a courageous militant who was committed to social change, and yet had the guts not to fight back, and he found that man in Robinson.

The first problems arose with the Dodger team itself. Several players, not just those of southern background, circulated a petition that they would not play with Robinson on the same field. Manager Leo Durocher ripped the players for their attitudes, and the Dodgers eventually got rid of those who could not overcome their racist attitudes.

But the worst invectives came from the opposing players and the fans in the stands. On one particularly bad day in Crosley Field against Cincinnati, Pee Wee Reese, a southerner, made a point of going over to Robinson and putting his arm around him, sending a clear message that they were teammates and friends. When his teammates stood up for Jackie, many of them became a part of the crusade for which Robinson was the figurehead, and it fused the Dodger ball club together in a special emotional way. This undoubtedly contributed to their winning the pennant almost every year. But they also had a great team.

With Robinson as the pioneering role model, almost all National League teams began the hunt for qualified black players, qualified meaning they had to *excel* at the game. No journeyman black need apply. So Milwaukee wound up with Henry Aaron, Chicago had Ernie Banks, Pittsburgh had Roberto Clemente, Cincinnati had Frank Robinson. And the Giants, of course, had Willie Mays. He was a little different from the other black stars. Mays radiated a boyish quality that differentiated him from Clemente and Robinson and Aaron, who gave the impression of being serious black men who were not just playing ball for the fun of it, but to excel, to be the best, and to beat you into the ground in the process.

Willie Mays managed to maintain the image of the boundless "natural" talent, even in the midst of serious racial provocations. In 1964 Mays's manager in San Francisco, Alvin Dark, gave an interview to a *Newsday* reporter in which he was quoted as saying: "We have trouble winning because we have so many Negro and Spanish-speaking ballplayers on this team. They are just not able to perform up to the white ballplayers when it comes to mental alertness." Mays, according to Dark, was the exception. The Giant roster at the time only included such people as Orlando Cepeda, Juan Marichal, and Willie McCovey, not to mention Jim Ray Hart, Jose Pagan, and Jesus and Matty Alou. Mays put down a full-scale mutiny in the clubhouse, and intervened behind the scenes to keep Dark from being fired, but he steered clear of the press, and remained free of controversy. This is not a criticism of Mays, because the priorities of a superstar are almost always to win games and keep his team together; gaining ground on social issues comes second.

Frank Robinson was in a position similar to Mays's with the great Orioles teams of the '60s. The Baltimore players, both black and white, would frequently go out together, but never at home. "I couldn't arrange black and white socializing in Baltimore even if it had been my nature to do that kind of thing," said Robinson. "I would have been afraid to. If I had invited teammates over to my house and one of the white players or his wife did not show up, it might have affected the Orioles as a ball club. I was always a team man above all else."

One black star of the '60s who went out of his way to transform his team into a real family was the Cardinals' Bob Gibson. The role he played for that ball club was very much at odds with the public's media image of Gibson. He was known as a player who didn't fraternize with opponents, who wouldn't even talk to teammates the day before he was going to pitch, and that was indeed true. But it was Gibson who repeatedly asked white players to join him and teammate Curt Flood after the game for a drink. Gibson overcame the fear that a white player might say no to an invitation, realizing that there was only one way to narrow the culture gap that separated the blacks from young whites like catcher Tim McCarver, who was from Tennessee, and that was to get to know each other. "When we got close to each other," said Flood, "we were able to inspire one another, and that was really the team's greatest attribute."

The proof of the special atmosphere on the Cardinals was the manner in which they brought players into the fold who had been unhappy for their whole careers, like Orlando Cepeda and Roger Maris. Cepeda had a reputation as a troublemaker with the Giants, but it was more a case of manager Alvin Dark rubbing him the wrong way. After Dark criticized black and Latin players for being "stupid" and "temperamental" and forbade the speaking of Spanish on team buses, Cepeda wound up being fingered as the ringleader of the team's overall discontent.

On the Cardinals, Cepeda found a team ready to welcome him and accept any eccentricity—he moved his stereo into the clubhouse, put on his favorite music, and the nickname "Cha Cha" was born. Cepeda returned the favor by dubbing the team "El Birdos." Responding to this overflowing goodwill, he won the 1967 MVP award.

For Roger Maris the problem wasn't race. In 1961 it was pure resentment for breaking the home-run record of the mythical Babe Ruth. He was never the same in New York after that, eventually souring on management when they let him play without telling him he had a broken hand. Maris was rejuvenated after being traded to St. Louis in 1967. "What makes it possible to continue," he said, "is the feeling on this Cardinal club. Everybody pulls for everybody else. It's a great club, close to a perfect club."

From the outside, Maris still had the image of a sullen, sulking, spoilsport; Cepeda was known as a volatile prima donna, and Gibson was branded as the impenetrable loner. On the Cardinals they participated in nothing less than baseball's version of the late '60s love-in. When the players took out their harmonicas and ukuleles and sang together to pass the time on the buses, they went far beyond the usual locker-room pranks and bawdy humor that passed for camaraderie on most teams. The Cardinals experienced something that was most rare in baseball, and when they talked about it with players from other teams, some were absolutely evangelical about it.

It was ironic, or perhaps fitting, that this interracial brotherhood among blacks, whites, and Latins should blossom in St. Louis, since the team probably had protested Jackie Robinson's entry into the majors more than any other franchise. Of course, this is not to say that the Cardinals' one-year blend of racial harmony and championship-level performance put an end to the tensions that sometimes crop up over the color of a teammate's skin. It will take a divine happening for color blindness to disappear in baseball or anywhere else. Until then, race will always be some kind of factor in the chemistry of the game. In 1989, for instance, outfielder Jeff Leonard, who was traded to the Brewers from the Giants, spoke out about the racial insensitivity of slugger Will Clark. He said Clark had called Chris Brown "a nigger" to his face in 1987, and had to apologize to the black players on the team. Then Leonard said that his brother asked

"The Thrill" for an autograph and Clark told him to buzz off. Leonard wanted to tear him apart right then, but said he resisted because the '87 playoffs were coming up and Leonard expected that he would hurt Clark if they fought. The story came to light when Clark told reporters that Leonard had been traded because he was a cancer on the team. When Leonard heard of Clark's remarks, he responded with his charges.

Baseball history has shown that talented teams can survive almost any kind of turmoil, if they've got the right stuff. The Oakland A's of the early '70s won three straight world championships, almost as a matter of course, despite constant internal feuding and profound interference from Oakland owner Charles O. Finley. Finley was a self-made man who became a millionaire by inventing a group insurance plan for doctors and then investing wisely in the stock market. He knew as much about sports as a career in the insurance business could teach him, and after years of trying to buy his way into baseball, he became the owner of the Kansas City Athletics in 1961.

Arrogant, persuasive, and unafraid to challenge baseball orthodoxy, Finley invited controversy. Jim Piersall once said he would write a book about his days with Finley and title it *And They Thought I Was Crazy*. Nearly twenty years later, however, it is stunning to consider how many of Finley's proposals have become commonplace. It was Finley who first recommended a designated hitter. It was Finley who pushed for weekday World Series games to be played at night, and the All-Star Game to be played at night as well, so working people could watch them. Finley also suggested a designated runner for the team's slowest man and a yellow baseball to be used for night games, but those ideas were considered too far out.

Finley was innovative with managers, too. In his eleven years at Kansas City, he had eleven of them. And he kept them all on a short leash. One of his managers, Joe Gordon, once even went to the plate with a lineup card signed "Approved by COF," the initials standing for Charles O. Finley. Onetime A's manager Dick Williams characterized Finley as someone who likes to have everyone "under his thumb," from the shoeshine boy to the manager. And then, Williams said, "he pushes as hard as he can to keep them down."

Finley regarded his players as commodities to promote, much like the mule, "Charley O," that he put in an A's cap and paraded through the streets of several cities. He gave pitcher Jim Hunter the nickname of "Catfish," which of course stuck with him throughout his Hall of Fame career. He even made up the story that created the fake nickname, a tall tale about little Jim coming home after having caught a mess o' catfish. Later he insisted that Vida Blue change his name to "True" Blue, but Vida resisted. Finley paid his players a bonus if they would grow mustaches or, at the very least, sideburns.

Finley finally met his match in arrogant swagger and prideful self-determination in a young slugger for the A's named Reggie Jackson. Jackson was emblematic of the new breed of black athletes who emerged in the wake of Muhammad Ali, Jim Brown, and Bill Russell—tough, independent, and unafraid to talk back. Jackson and Finley engaged in a protracted war of wills, through holdouts over money, benchings, and fights in the press. On at least one occasion, Jackson homered, then shook his fist up at the owner's box when he returned to home plate, while mouthing things that the beat writers could never print.

The A's still managed to win, even when Finley had the team ready to walk out on the World Series, as nearly happened in 1973 after the Mike Andrews incident. Andrews, normally a fine fielder, booted two grounders in the twelfth inning to blow a game against the New York Mets. Finley wanted him out of the Series so bad that he brought Andrews into the trainer's room with manager Williams and the team doctor, and pressured Andrews into signing a fake medical report that he was hurt. The team was told that he had a sore shoulder, but when they found out the truth, they were hopping mad.

Reggie Jackson said, "I've never seen the mood of a team so mean. We're near to mutiny. Some of the guys want to follow Mike and walk right out of the World Series." The commissioner turned down Finley's request to add a healthy player for Andrews, and when Andrews's name was announced in New York, he received a standing ovation.

Trailing 3–2 in the Series, the A's came back to Oakland and rallied to win another championship. Blue Moon Odom said it all, yelling in the clubhouse: "Dissension does it again."

One sportswriter suggested that Finley deserved credit for stirring the team up. "Please don't give that man the credit," said Reggie Jackson. "That takes away from what the guys have done. It would have been the easiest thing in the world for this team to lie down because of what that man did. He spoiled what should have been a beautiful thing. We went on and did what we could do because we have character."

Even when Finley was not riling up the troops, the Athletics' blend of volatile personalities supplied plenty of fireworks. The 1974 season, for instance, was not exactly a sunny campaign. Alvin Dark took over from Dick Williams as manager and began introducing Bible quotations and prayer sessions into the clubhouse on a daily basis. Team captain Sal Bando stood up one day and told the team: "Alvin Dark couldn't manage a meat market." But the A's continued to win, and to fight.

After a game in which center fielder Bill North was publicly chewed out by Jackson for not running out a ground ball, the two players didn't speak for a month. Their strained relationship was exacerbated by an incident involving a woman. Jackson's version: "I had introduced him to a girl. Then one night at a bar when he wasn't around, the girl started coming on to me. I sort of brushed her off, but when the story got back to North, it was Reggie who had come on to the girl and not vice versa."

Before a game in Detroit, North accused Jackson of trying to "steal his woman" and called him "a faggot." They leaped on each other, swinging. Vida Blue and John Odom tried to pull the two men apart. Catcher Ray Fosse also played peacemaker, wanting to protect Blue from getting hurt. Fosse was himself wrestled off his feet and thrown back against a locker. Minutes after they were separated, they began trading punches again. North was considerably smaller than Jackson, but he had his clothes on and won the second round, knocking Jackson down heavily on his right shoulder.

The battle had its repercussions. Fosse thought he had a crick in his neck and tried to shake it off, actually catching most of the game before the pain between his shoulders grew too intense. He was flown back to Oakland, where he was put in traction, then operated on to repair a ruptured cervical disc. Fosse didn't play again until

September, and the battle just about ended his career. But he said he had no regrets. "When you see two guys fighting on your club, you say to yourself, 'Hey, they're messing with my money.' " The game the night of the North-Jackson bout was won by the A's 9–1.

Clubhouse fighting and feuding seemed to intensify the Athletics' winning spirit. In the 1974 World Series, Blue Moon Odom got into a fight with Rollie Fingers. It seems that Odom had made some disparaging remark about Fingers's wife, and they began throwing grocery carts at each other. Ray Fosse didn't want anything to do with it: "I broke into a cold sweat and ran into the trainer's room, fearing I was gonna get caught up in another one and get something else broken."

Another time it was Campy Campaneris and Vida Blue going at it, but it was no sweat for this team, which used to joke about their routine—batting practice, brawling, take infield, and then play the game and win. "When a fight would break out in the A's clubhouse," said Jackson, "no one would even look up from their card games. You'd just be sort of bemused."

When Reggie compared the Athletics' championship dynasty of '72–74 with the current team that won pennants from '88 to '90, he said that a team gets its personality from its owner. "We were a reflection of Finley. He was volatile, abrasive, and combative. We fed off that. The current A's team is very businesslike, just like the Haas family which owns it."

Far from being swashbuckling, firing-from-the-hip renegades, the A's under owner Walter Haas and manager Tony LaRussa can be characterized by their cool professionalism. Aside from the outspoken José Canseco making the papers for his speeding tickets or nocturnal visits with Madonna, or Rickey Henderson insisting that a Ferrari be thrown in with his contract, they have been a low-key franchise.

It was not until the A's had been beaten by the Reds in the first two games of the 1990 World Series that Oakland revealed any of the turmoil and infighting that made their dynastic ancestors such a success. Canseco had failed to make a catch in right field on a fly ball that allowed the Reds to tie Game Two in the eighth inning. After the game, LaRussa refused to make excuses for Canseco, who happened not to be at full strength with a bad back. The manager said that the ball was catchable, that Canseco didn't get a good jump and he didn't know why he didn't, and that if he was not healthy enough to play, he'd be benched.

Nobody could remember another time that LaRussa had publicly criticized one of his ballplayers. The verbal potshots appeared to be a ploy, a way of firing up José and the team. But then, as the Series shifted to Oakland, LaRussa and Canseco downplayed the comments, had a long chat, and assured the media that they were the best of friends. So the 1990 edition of the A's went out all lovey-dovey in Game Three and got wiped up again by the Reds, effectively ending their bid to repeat as world champions by putting them down three games to none.

And yet another major league team, the New York Yankees, had a Finley of their own, and then some, George Steinbrenner, but there was no dynasty for that team.

The key question comes down to this—why are some teams destroyed by backbiting, resentment, jealousy, and bad chemistry, while other teams take out their frustrations consistently on their opponents? Willie Randolph, who was involved in plenty of turmoil playing with Steinbrenner's Yankees, said, "It's a matter of what kinds of players you're talking about. We had Munson, Nettles, Chambliss, Gossage, Guidry, Jackson—all guys who could deal with it." Some players are just able to focus on the athletic and mental demands of a baseball game no matter what's happening in the press, with the owner, with their manager, or with their teammates—and even with wives. Pete Rose used to brag about how well he hit during his divorce. And Keith Hernandez also went on a hot streak while his divorce was being finalized. He said that if he got divorced more often he'd be in the Hall of Fame, but he'd also be broke. For a player like Hernandez, the field was the only place where he was free. He never had a problem concentrating: "Baseball," he said, "is my meditation."

What is playing ball, after all, but the ability to meditate for three hours? Playing baseball well, even for the most seasoned veteran, is a matter of continually reminding yourself what to do in ever-changing situations. Preparedness and attention are all, despite the mind's inclination to wander during long at-bats or lulls in the action. This heightened focus can bring a kind of freedom, because the player becomes embedded in the game's flow. In a trancelike cocoon, he is free of life's cares. He is safely inside the games within the games.

The Mets' Chemistry Test

There are undoubtedly special pressures that come with playing baseball in New York, and most have to do with the wealth of media concerns. Making up the media locally are four major daily newspapers and twenty-four-hour-a-day sports-talk radio discussions, radio and television game announcers, networks and magazines who lavish special attention on the New York sports scene.

Just what can such pressure do to a player? Bill Robinson came up with the Yankees in the '60s, hit a home run in his second at-bat, and was stunned to find fifty news people crowded around his locker. His New York playing experience was not a success, however. He wound up with the Pirates, a late bloomer who knew he would have developed sooner as a player if he had started his career anywhere but in New York. As the hitting instructor for the Mets in 1989, Robinson vicariously relived his early baseball life in New York, dispassionately experiencing the hang-ups of three terminally slumping Mets—Gregg Jefferies, Darryl Strawberry, and Juan Samuel. "It's the people who learn to relax here who are the ones who become stars," Robinson said. "I don't think you can ever measure if players can handle New York before you bring them here."

Yankee MSG announcer Tony Kubek doesn't believe that "New York pressures" can derail a whole ball club. "I think the media can have an effect on an individual player who might crack under the microscope," he said, "but a talented team can override that kind of criticism of one guy."

Mike Francesa of New York's all-sports radio station WFAN emphasized that there are other places where the pressure makes it as tough to perform. "Ask Mike Schmidt about playing in Philadelphia. Or ask a Denver Bronco about playing in Denver. Ask John Elway. To one extent, it's lessened here because we have so many pro teams. If you have only one pro team, it's examined and reexamined 365 days a year."

But the intense sports coverage in the media capital of the country is daunting. As soon as the first pitch is thrown in the baseball season, the sports establishment seems to take a collective deep breath in preparation for blowing things totally out of proportion. Was it a coincidence that the 1978 Yankees made their astounding run to the pennant under Bob Lemon and overtook the Red Sox in the midst of a newspaper strike that lasted for months? That fortuitous blackout masked the team's internal strife, which featured the shoving match between Reggie Jackson and Billy Martin on national television; indeed, the strike may have helped allow the team's considerable talent to shine through.

The powerhouse Yankees of an earlier era, the late '50s and early '60s, generally treated the press as invaders in the clubhouse. Mickey Mantle, for one, was surly with writers in those days, although his friend Whitey Ford was quite open with the press. A young pitcher named Jim Bouton was the one Yankee who liked to have the press crowd around his locker, but that made him something of an outcast on the team even before he crossed the line of clubhouse confidentiality with *Ball Four*.

Coverage of the New York Mets, meanwhile, evolved in a different way entirely. The departure of the Dodgers and Giants to the golden West had left an aching void. So writers as well as the fans were delighted to have a National League team playing in New York once again. In the early '60s, a number of sportswriters came on the scene who were of a new generation. They carried very little of the imperious baggage of the old-guard sportswriters who looked down on the field like wizened oracles and wrote reviews of the game as if they were theater critics. These new journalists—Phil Pepe, George Vecsey, Larry Merchant, Stan Isaacs, among others—earned the name "chipmunks" from the veteran sportswriters. These were writers who often took a lighter, more detached approach to covering sports. These traffickers in irreverence got the perfect opportunity to display the new sports gestalt when the Mets were created in 1962.

Casey Stengel, the Mets' first manager and renowned manipulator of the press, took the writers under his wing, and set the tone for the season. When the Mets lost, Casey would tell the writers funny stories in Stengelese from his long career. On the rare occasions when they won, he would let veteran players like Roger Craig, Richie Ashburn, and Frank Thomas joke about winning the pennant.

This expansion team was truly one of the worst in baseball history. That first spring in Florida, a visiting journalist asked Howard Cosell how the Mets were shaping up, and received a patented Cosell reply: "It's enough to strain the credulity of a rational man."

The fans got into it right away and went to the old Polo Grounds to see Marv Throneberry miss first base, or cringe when fielders collided like bumper cars under a pop-up, or witness a game-losing wild pitch in the ninth inning—things they could tell their grandchildren about. It was the first time a horrible team was covered so gently. Maury Allen was reporting the Mets for the *New York Post,* his first baseball beat. He remembers, "It became a matter of the writers trying to outdo each other by being funnier than the others."

When Gil Hodges took over as Mets manager in 1968, the first thing he had to straighten out with the writers was that he didn't think losing ballgames was all that funny. But even when the Mets became a world championship team the following year, the original standard still applied. The players and reporters got on famously. "The '69 Mets," said Maury Allen, "were as close to the press as any team in history." Allen admitted that he and a lot of the other chipmunks rooted hard for that team.

Within a year or two of that World Series victory, things began to change. Free agency was already percolating in the courts. Salaries suddenly began escalating dramatically. It was then that the relationship between writers and athletes changed drastically. Ballplayers making several hundred thousand dollars a year were on a different level financially from the writers, and this, along with the wedding of sport with television, strained the relationship between player and writer.

The athletes became minicorporations who generally had their own self-interest at heart. As *Newsday*'s Stan Isaacs, one of the original chipmunks, said, "Politicians feel that they have some responsibility to the public, however crooked they are. Ballplayers don't feel they have any responsibility to the public. They look upon the press as somebody to help them, not to get at the truth."

Of course, it's a two-way street, and the writers also approached the athletes with their own ends in mind. In an effort to make names for themselves and sell newspapers, many baseball writers for the tabloids followed the lead of Dick Young, an influential columnist with the *Daily News*. In his later years, Young became increasingly critical of players like Tom Seaver for trying to get more money. Young often created friction for the sake of a hard-hitting story. The Mets' trading of Seaver in 1977 was due in no small part to Young's repeated bashings of the Mets' star pitcher over his hold-outs.

Today the sports pages in New York, except possibly those of *The New York Times,* must have what sportswriter and editor Vic Ziegel terms "back pages that vibrate." The result is that New York teams have to play in a media hailstorm that presents a season as a weepy and tumultuous soap opera. The successful players in New York have been those with the ego strength to ignore most of the outside influences—Dave Winfield, for one; Reggie Jackson for another.

Consider what Dave Righetti endured from the media during his ten years in New York, in which he changed over from a starter who once pitched a no-hitter to a successful but often-maligned relief pitcher. Time and again the New York sporting press set him up to be traded or supplanted by another pitcher as the Yankees' bullpen closer, until he left to sign on with the San Francisco Giants for the 1991 season.

"Rags," a man with a temper to begin with (he once threw a ball completely out of the stadium when being taken out of a game he had blown), recalls that the worst beatings he took in the press came on the road, hearing about back-page headlines like "Rags in Tatters" or some such nicety.

Somewhat wearily, Righetti took the rabid sports coverage in stride, accepting it as the baseball cross he had to bear. "It's run people out of town," he said, "and it's made other people better than they were. Obviously, the press likes to think they can make or break you, but your abilities will make or break you. If you do let these things get to you, they'll know it and smell it and they'll try to dig into you."

The Mets' case history, especially in recent years, shows how a franchise tries to cope with media pressure. The Mets' triumvirate of executives—general manager Frank Cashen, former director of baseball operations Joe McIlvaine, and vice president Al Harazin—put their winning teams together in the '80s by acquiring players who they felt had the mental toughness to handle this constant pressure. Keith Hernandez, Gary Carter, Howard Johnson, and Kevin McReynolds were all acquired in trades, and all them were available because they were considered problems of one sort or another with their former teams. They were players toughened by criticism for either hogging the headlines, like Carter in Montreal; or drug abuse and nonhustle, like Hernandez in St. Louis; or immaturity and selfishness, like Johnson in Detroit; or just general indifference, like McReynolds in San Diego.

The very qualities that enabled these men to succeed in the howling den of New York's impatient fans and press also made the Mets an unpopular bunch outside of New York. Former Montreal Expos manager Bob Rodgers pointed out why nobody in the National League East used to root for the Mets. "There's an arrogance, a standoffishness, that you have to have playing in New York because there's so many phonies around all the time, and it carries onto the field."

The organization's practice of collecting talented players who didn't quite fit in with their former teams and plunking them down in the pressure cooker of New York actually worked for the Mets. Davey Johnson always said that he didn't mind selfish players as long as they did their jobs. These players presented no problems on a winning team, and the Mets thrived as the club that fans across the country loved to hate. But in the years after their 1986 World Series win, the team was often beset by bickering, apparent disinterest in fundamentals, and the kind of malaise that deeply worried management—in short, sour chemistry.

The first symbol of the Mets going astray was Dwight Gooden's flirtation with cocaine. After their *Wunderkind* starting ace went into drug rehab in 1987, the Mets had his counselor at the Smithers Alcoholism Treatment and Training Center in Manhattan, Dr. Allan Lans, accompany the team. The doctor's presence was part of Gooden's aftercare program, and eventually the Mets appointed Dr. Lans as their year-round psychiatrist.

The Mets joined five other major league teams that employ psychologists or psychiatrists to help their players cope on at least a semiregular basis. The Athletics have Harvey Dorfman, and the Indians have Rick Wolff, psychologists whom they classify as "special instructors." Wolff is a former minor league player, and Dorfman coauthored the book, *The Mental Game of Baseball.* The Orioles and Expos use psychologists without a baseball background, while the Phillies, along with the Mets, use psychiatrists.

In a business sense, these specialists are there to protect the investments of the owners by helping in the prevention and treatment of drug abuse or domestic unrest, or simply a bad case of the blahs. And in the wake of the championship season, the Mets' head doctor had to work overtime, as one Met after another became in his turn a bundle of nerves and frustrations.

The 1987 season featured a devastating number of pitching injuries, and the Mets still nearly overtook the Cardinals. But in 1988 came the turning point: after winning their division, the Mets suffered a crushing seventh-game playoff loss to Orel Hershiser and the Dodgers. The following spring, the scars had not yet healed. There were yearlong eruptions of all kinds—from jealousy over playing time and salary, to fights with columnists, broadcasters, and fans, to problems with team leadership, as well as questions about the manager's control of the team.

Even the role of the team shrink came under fire near the end of the '89 season. Shortly before he was traded, Randy Myers, the Mets' Rambo reliever, complained that his teammates would go to Dr. Lans when they had a problem instead of talking it out with other players. He thought the arrangement led to estrangement. Tim Teufel was another Met who thought Lans was too involved in the players' affairs. "I don't think we need a psychiatrist to win ballgames." Some players had a hard time accepting the fact that their talks behind closed doors with a private consultant were truly confidential. "I have no doubt that he's ethical," said pitcher David Cone, "but he's hired by management, they sign his checks. It's a classic labor-versus-management situation."

Of course, Dr. Lans cannot reveal what went on in his sessions with the players. But if his presence was salutary for the ball club, what did he prevent from happening? The truth is that every "people problem" the Mets feared could erupt during the 1989 season—the crisis of team leadership as Carter and Hernandez became lame ducks, getting players to accept reduced roles, an inability to motivate Strawberry, the failure to integrate Gregg Jefferies into the clubhouse—blew up in their faces.

When the Mets failed to shake themselves out of the doldrums in 1990, the organization decided to make a change. Two months into the '90 season, Davey Johnson, the winningest manager of his generation, was fired and replaced by Buddy Harrelson. After the season, Joe McIlvaine, the Mets' director of baseball operations, known as one of the shrewdest player-personnel executives in baseball, left to take the GM job in San Diego. And Darryl Strawberry signed on with the Dodgers. In many respects these changes marked the end of an era for the Mets.

Fairly or not, many observers characterized the Met ball clubs of the '80s as underachievers, but only because they had contended so consistently, like the Blue Jays and Red Sox, without winning it all. For seven years straight, from 1984 to 1990, the Mets finished no worse than second, and won ninety games every one of those years except for '89. But the glory of their championship season made others pale by comparison. "We're cursed by 1986," said executive vice president Al Harazin, "but those kinds of years don't happen too often." As former coach and new manager Buddy Harrelson put it, "We're all disappointed that we haven't won more championships. Nobody cares who finished second."

The seven turbulent seasons that Darryl Strawberry played in Flushing, Queens, before the faithful at Shea Stadium in many ways were a mirror of the performance of the ball club: while his accomplishments were impressive, there was always the nagging sense that he had somehow not lived up to his potential. Strawberry was hyped from high school days as the "black Ted Williams." Projections of fifty-homer seasons were made not only by the media but by Darryl himself. As Davey Johnson put it, "I was really proud of his effort, although he probably was never able to accept whatever he gave because he felt he was always short of people's expectations."

When Strawberry had a big year in 1988, hitting thirty-nine home runs for the second year in a row, he desperately wanted the MVP award to certify that he had truly arrived. But Kirk Gibson, in recognition of the leadership qualities he provided for the Dodgers, won the award despite fourteen fewer homers and twenty-five fewer RBIs. Strawberry's feelings were hurt, and he was doubly wounded when Keith Hernandez said that Kevin McReynolds, because of his consistency, had been the Most Valuable Met.

The following spring, Strawberry held out to have his contract renegotiated, since he was, after the signings of Kevin McReynolds, Ron Darling, and Howard Johnson, unhappily the fifth-highest paid player on the team. But the front office refused, and Strawberry arrived in Port St. Lucie, Florida, the converted swampland that serves as the Mets' training camp, with a skyscraper-sized chip on his shoulder. He was feeling, justly or unjustly, totally unappreciated, the neglected child.

Keith Hernandez had played the role of both booster and critic to Strawberry, and the two had a close but complicated relationship. When the players posed for the team picture on Photo Day, an exasperated Hernandez said, "Oh, grow up, you big crybaby," and Strawberry snapped. He went after Keith and threw a left, yelling, "I'm tired of your shit. I've been tired of you for years."

It was the beginning of a disastrous season for Strawberry, which damaged relations with his manager, teammates, the press, and the fans. He was atrocious in the outfield, and disappeared at the plate. He finished the year with a .225 batting average, hitting .053 (one for nineteen) with runners in scoring position in the late innings of close games.

After the season, Strawberry's saga took another dramatic turn.

He was arrested in Los Angeles for allegedly threatening to shoot his wife, Lisa, with a handgun at the end of a domestic quarrel in January 1990. Just two days before, blood tests had established that Strawberry was the father of another woman's baby, which could not have helped Darryl and Lisa's reconciliation. Soon after his arrest, he checked into an alcohol rehab program at the Smithers Center in New York.

Dr. Lans was instrumental in getting Strawberry to seek treatment for his alcohol problem, which Darryl later attributed to the pressures and expectations thrust upon him. Met management admitted that if it were not for their team psychiatrist, Strawberry would not have sought help. "No," said Al Harazin, "I don't think any of us could have convinced Darryl to get help. We're still the people's employer. We are the representative of the man who signs people's checks. That's just the way it is."

Strawberry had reached a crossroads in his baseball career, and to his credit he responded with a massive 1990 campaign—thirty-seven homers and 108 RBIs, not to mention his vastly improved play in the outfield. Unfortunately, there was a year-long distraction about how many millions he was worth to the organization. General manager Frank Cashen put it bluntly in mid-season when he said that Strawberry was not worth the $5 million per year that José Canseco had just signed for: "We have to stop talking about potential. What we have here is a pretty good ballplayer."

After the snub, Strawberry cooled off as a hitter. As one of his running buddies, pitcher David Cone, said, "Just when he would get locked in, there was always something to knock him off track, either in his personal life or his contract." Dwight Gooden agreed. "Darryl would hit a three-run home run in the ninth inning to win a game for us. But the minute he got back in the clubhouse, people would be asking, 'Are you leaving?' and Darryl would get mad all over again."

Did Strawberry get a fair shake from the New York media, the Mets management, and the fans? Few players of his stature have been both booed so loudly and cheered so wildly. New York's fans, among the most knowledgeable in the country, take bad baseball as a personal insult, and more often than not, like to demonstrate their displeasure. During the summer of the 1986 championship season, Strawberry was booed at Shea Stadium so regularly that he wound up hitting one hundred points below his road average. "It's disgusting the way the fans treat me in New York," he said at the time. "They like to point the finger at one particular player and say he's not doing well. It's not fair for a player to suffer through that."

But there were reasons for the frustrations of the fans as well as the media after watching Strawberry day after day in the outfield. He appeared nonchalant, catching everything one-handed. While he is such a tall and graceful athlete that he can run very fast without looking as if he's hustling, at other times during the '89 season he did look lazy.

Strawberry only made one play well in the outfield, when he leaped at the fence to rob somebody of a home run. There you saw his timing, coordination, and athletic ability come to the fore. But he didn't get a good jump on the ball, and even though he had a powerful arm, he took extra steps and therefore too much time to release his throws. And he did miss the cutoff man a lot of times. He also couldn't pick up fly balls in the sun, couldn't play on wet grass, and didn't charge base hits. There was little indication that he worked on his defense at all.

The carping of Met TV broadcaster Tim McCarver on Strawberry's fielding reached crisis dimensions by the end of the '89 season. McCarver based his criticism on the fact that Darryl played everybody in virtually the same place, whether it be a powerful left-handed hitter or a weak right-handed hitter. He played everybody deep, in a spot, grown brown by midsummer, that habitués seated along the right-field line referred to as "the Strawberry Patch." It got to the point where McCarver told Darryl face-to-face that he was too good an athlete to be afraid to go back on the ball. Darryl, by way of reply, just stared back at him.

Strawberry was the most sensitive of superstars when it came to criticism. As his friend Eric Davis said, "Darryl hears everything. He reads a lot of stuff and takes a lot of it personally." As far as the press was concerned, it seemed that Strawberry never accepted the fact that the same people who had anointed him as a demigod when he was going good would tear him down when he didn't hit. During one protracted cold spell in '89, Strawberry adopted a bunker mentality, blaming his slump on the media, and he stopped talking to the press.

It was easy for Strawberry to think that whatever he did wasn't good enough for the Mets' top brass, his manager, his teammates, the writers, or the fans. Hadn't he hit some big home runs for this team? What about the dinger that hit the clock in St. Louis off Ken Daley in extra innings to win a crucial pitching duel between Ron Darling and John Tudor 1–0 in the last days of the 1985 regular season? Or the homer in game five of the '86 playoffs off Nolan Ryan to send that game to extra innings, or for that matter his three-run homer off Bob Knepper in game three of the same storied playoff?

Yet Strawberry was routinely downgraded for his inconsistency and not being a better clutch hitter. It's hard to argue with the power numbers that Strawberry put up; they compare favorably with the statistics that New York legends like Snider, Mantle, and Mays produced in their first full seven seasons. And each of those Hall of Famers played in better hitter's parks than the Met slugger.

Strawberry's own teammates, even as they recognized his considerable talents, seem not to have fully appreciated his presence in the clubhouse. As soon as he left, teammates grumbled that he wouldn't play hurt, wouldn't take treatment for his injuries, even that he was drinking again. So it should not be surprising that as the 1991 season began, most players on the Mets were looking forward to the new atmosphere in Year One A.D. (After Darryl). "He put himself above the team," said Dave Magadan. "Last year, Darryl got all the credit when we played well and he was quick to accept it."

If the front office meant to send a message to the players by allowing Strawberry to leave, Gregg Jefferies received it loud and clear: "Now we know we have to come together." But that winning blend of talent and commitment has become an increasingly difficult proposition for the Mets since their world championship team.

From the time Davey Johnson took over as manager in 1984, he always gave his players a great deal of responsibility. It would only be a slight exaggeration to say that in his first years he let Keith Hernandez handle the internal politics of the team, let Gary Carter handle the pitchers, and sat back while the Mets enjoyed the nightlife of Manhattan. But as the team proved mortal, Johnson was criticized for letting his players get away with too much. Then came what he called "my most embarrassing moment in managing," the night in September of '89 when Strawberry and McReynolds were undressing in the clubhouse while the team was rallying against Chicago in the ninth inning.

After the '89 season, Joe McIlvaine, for one, pressed to have Johnson fired. "I thought Davey had become a recluse," McIlvaine explained. "He was too distant from the players." Cashen, who had waffled about having Johnson return for the 1990 season, finally decided to give Johnson another chance. He was kept on as the manager for 1990 with the proviso that he would have to be more of a disciplinarian; he knew he had to prove the club could still win under him.

Instead of getting off to a fast start in 1990, the Mets committed errors, allowed a tremendous number of stolen bases, and failed to hit with runners on base. The hitters were at their worst with a man on third base and less than two out. They scored only when they hit home runs, and the rest of the time looked anemic. The bench players groused about their lack of playing time, and the regulars castigated the bench players for not rooting for them while they lost game after game. Team meetings were held about the club's flagging spirit, all to no avail.

And then came the fiasco in Atlanta. David Cone took a throw from first baseman Mike Marshall to complete a 3–1 putout, catching the base with the side of his foot. The umpire called the runner safe, and Cone exploded in disbelief. There were runners on first and second when the play began. Dale Murphy scored while Cone argued, and so did Ernie Whitt, who runs like he's dragging a batting cage behind him. All of this occurred a full *twenty seconds* after the close call at first. Cone was so out of it he didn't even know which Met was screaming at him and trying to get the ball out of his glove. The headlines were typical: "Conehead the Bonehead," etc. In the end it was but another indictment of the Davey Johnson regime.

By May, the Mets were struggling big-time. Johnson sacrificed more defense in one game at Shea by putting Howard Johnson at shortstop.

Hojo made three errors, and after the Reds stole four bases in one inning, the manager came out to get his pitcher and heard the full-throated chant for the first time from the disgruntled home fans: "Davey must go!"

Second-guessing the manager became a habit among the players. One night in San Francisco they were beaten by Gary Carter's game-winning single against Bob Ojeda. The players felt Johnson should have brought in a righty reliever. After a couple of beers that night, four Mets were in front of the hotel when a homeless man approached, asking for money. "Hey, Davey," one of the Mets said to the beggar, "you should've brought in a right-hander."

In the middle of May, the struggling Strawberry tried to console Johnson. "Don't worry, Skip," he said. "I'm going to come around." And Johnson said, "I hope you do it before I get fired."

Before May was over, Johnson was gone, hustled out a side door of the Cincinnati Hilton, not given the chance to say good-bye to the players. Cashen just "disappeared" him. Later, Johnson admitted that he had to go. "It was the best thing for the organization because the situation was hurting the chemistry."

Enter Buddy Harrelson, longtime Met shortstop and coach. He instituted some new rules—no playing golf on game days, no card-playing in the clubhouse, mandatory stretching exercises before batting practice. They were hardly the decrees of Captain Bligh, but at least they symbolized the new regime. Compared to Johnson's *laissez-faire* style, Harrelson was a Great Communicator. As Tim Teufel put it, "Davey communicated with his lineup card." "A lot of players here," said Frank Viola, who joined the Mets in '89, "needed a little babying and caressing, and Buddy could talk to them."

In an effort to motivate Strawberry, Harrelson had him take the lineup card to the umpires. He reminded his star that he didn't have to be a vocal leader in the clubhouse, but to do his talking with the bat. Strawberry had wanted to maintain the "inner peace" he had found at Smithers. He said he had lost some of the "dirty dog" he had in him once he stopped drinking. He told Harrelson he would get mad at the pitcher, but then hold it in. "Don't hold it in," Harrelson told Strawberry.

What followed was an eighteen-game hitting streak during which

Strawberry hit .412 with nine homers and twenty-four RBIs. By the end of June, the Mets were only one game behind the Pirates, and looked more than formidable. But it proved to be a mirage, as the team's weaknesses were exposed. Unreliable setup relief pitching, a thin bench, and weak hitting in the clutch doomed Harrelson's moves to backfire. The Mets failed to play well on the road, their record against left-handed starters wound up as the worst in the league (27–33), and the team was only 14–25 in games decided by one or two runs.

The honeymoon over, Harrelson became known as a manager who made tactical moves strictly by the book, and on several occasions, it led players to rebel against the Buddy System.

One of those moves in September made pitcher David Cone absolutely livid. Despite his celebrated vapor lock in Atlanta, Cone was one of the best second-half pitchers in baseball in 1990. In a game against Philadelphia Cone had struck out twelve Phillies by the seventh inning and had a one-run lead when he faced Len Dykstra with a runner on second. When Harrelson checked his "book," he saw that Dykstra was 4–12 off Cone, and 0–4 against lefty reliever Jeff Musselman. However, Cone was dominant that night, and Musselman had struggled all season (in fact, Harrelson himself once joked that Musselman, after a stint in the minors to straighten out his mechanics, would be back with the team because he had the best-looking wife on the club). Harrelson took out Cone and brought in Musselman, who gave up three straight hits—and the ballgame.

In a big matchup with the first-place Pirates in September at Pittsburgh, Harrelson tabbed rookie Julio Valera for his first big-league start. Valera got bombed. Passing over veteran pitchers Ron Darling and Bob Ojeda in that game mystified much of the team, and led to wholesale second-guessing of the manager. Some wondered if Harrelson was just a figurehead for the desires of management. Harrelson felt the repercussions in the clubhouse, and it bothered him as he watched the pennant slip away. "My hair's not falling out," he said down the stretch, "but it *is* getting grayer."

And so the Mets finished second again, but in the process made several important moves to reshape the team. The key player in that transition continued to be Gregg Jefferies, as the Met brain trust struggled to find a position for him. In the minors, where he was a two-time Minor League Player of the Year, he played shortstop. That was the organization's first mistake with him. Jefferies hit so impressively in his late-season debut in 1988 that the Mets planned to trade Howard Johnson in spring training of 1989 and give third base to Jefferies. When they failed to make that trade, the Mets wound up putting Jefferies at second base, which is an "experience-preferred" position in the big leagues.

Davey Johnson, a former second baseman, took on the task of making Jefferies into a second-sacker, where he received on-the-job-training during the 1989 season. His awkwardness in the field was thus expected, but everybody, including Jefferies, expected him to hit. He was, however, desperately overanxious from the get-go, displaying none of the savvy he had shown in his late-season call-up the previous year. And he reacted badly to it, taking to throwing his helmet and bat, punching water coolers, and cursing himself constantly, as if he only cared about himself and not the team. His teammates thought he was putting a little too much importance on his own play, and shunned him for his unprofessional comportment.

After the season, Davey Johnson did indeed confront his prize rookie about his pouting. "I told him, 'If I see it one more time, I'll get your butt out of here.' He was looking like it was the end of the world all the time. And what really ticked me off is when Gregg would walk back real slow after making an out. It bothered me and I'm sure it bothered the players. But you know what? Once I said that to him, he stopped. I think there was a lot of petty jealousy toward him. The resentment was overdone. If I thought it would help Gregg to go down, I would've sent him out. But I didn't want to break Gregg's spirit, and I was willing to get fired over it."

Jefferies's monomaniacal obsession with hitting also grated on his teammates, like his habit of asking umpires in the field what was wrong with his swing. In the locker room, he spent all his time polishing his bats. In July Jefferies spent so long stroking and cleaning his wood that it had to be packed among the uniforms. When Jefferies showered, Strawberry pulled the bat out and threw it disdainfully across the clubhouse.

"I had nobody, except for [Lee] Mazzilli and Carter," Jefferies recalled. "I wouldn't wish that year on anyone." As late as June of '89, Jefferies was still only hitting .182. He was getting conflicting advice from players, writers, and fans, but worst of all he was caught in a crossfire between the Mets' hitting instructor, Bill Robinson, and his own father, who had been his confidant and batting teacher throughout his career.

Jefferies finally turned it around in the last six weeks of the '89 season, hitting .355 with eight homers in his last twenty-two games. His relations with the rest of the team improved in his second full season. Leading the league with forty doubles in 1990 was a good way of winning respect. But several Mets remained cool to Jefferies. He was tolerated, but remained an outsider even as he tried to fit in. As one veteran Met put it, "I don't think we'll ever really like Gregg."

When third baseman Howard Johnson performed surprisingly well at shortstop during the latter half of the 1990 season, the Mets continued the infield musical chairs by putting Jefferies back at third. But then Hojo made a ton of errors at short early in the '91 season, and had to be repositioned at third base. So Jefferies was back at second, where he hadn't taken a grounder all spring, with predictably ugly consequences—miscues that blew ballgames.

The open resentment of Jefferies resurfaced in the clubhouse, and he responded to the slings and arrows with an open letter that was read over the local sports-talk radio station. In effect, he pleaded with the fans, the press, and his teammates to get off his back and let him play baseball because all he wanted to do was win. But if he really did not want to be characterized as an immature whiner, this embarrassing missive was not the answer.

The "Jefferies problem" was just one of the things that the players themselves were apprehensive about going into the 1991 season. In the post-Strawberry era, the Mets knew they would have to find new ways to win. They had two new outfielders, speedster Vince Coleman and Hubie Brooks. Coleman gave the Mets a legitimate leadoff man, and Brooks provided a sorely needed right-handed RBI bat that promised to give the batting order better balance. So management filled some very serious holes, even with the loss of Strawberry. As Harazin stressed, "Veterans like Coleman, Brooks, and Tommie Herr can fit into any team they're on."

Certainly the lineup would have a different feel from the big-bang offenses the Mets had put together in years past. Brooks, returning to New York for the first time since 1984, felt the Mets would need contributions from everyone on the roster to win. "Nobody," said Harrelson, "will be waiting for someone to hit thirty-seven homers. I'm just making them more conscious of the other ways of winning a ballgame, pushing a runner and scoring without a base hit."

The Mets were singing a very different tune from those teams that used to go into each season as the consensus pick to win, and proclaim that it should be easy, too—that they should dominate. Just about every player wondered about how the new pieces of the puzzle would fit together in 1991. "I'm anxious to see what we have," said Gooden in spring training. "I've been trying to figure if we're a great team or a good team, and you just don't know. It can go either way."

Gooden and Ron Darling, as the senior Mets in terms of continuous service to the ball club, had seen plenty of changes in the team's interpersonal dynamics. "I've been on teams that got along," said Darling, "and I've been on clubs that bitched and moaned at each other. I don't know what's better."

When Strawberry left, it marked the exit of the very last regular everyday player from the Mets' 1986 championship team. That arrogant, defiant, swaggering, take-that, in-your-face ball club—with Dykstra, Backman, Knight, Mitchell, Carter, Hernandez, and the rest—had a very dynamic mix of personalities compared with the lower-keyed players who now populated the Met clubhouse. "Nobody on that team," recalled Gooden, "was afraid to high-five a guy or hold his hand up to the crowd. We've gotten more laid-back, less outspoken. When the heat was on, those guys in '86 got pumped up. The question is how these players here respond when we have a slump."

Darling, on the other hand, didn't think the '86 team was that extraordinary. "We had the same guys in '87 and it wasn't special. The '86 team is glorified because we won and had an awesome playoff and World Series." This brings us back to the chicken and the egg:

Leo Durocher and umpire George Magerkurth were always battling.

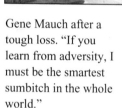

If you referred to legendary large-lipped umpire Bill Klem by his nickname, "Catfish," you were gone for the day.

Gene Mauch after a tough loss. "If you learn from adversity, I must be the smartest sumbitch in the whole world."

Don Zimmer giving the ump an animated earful.

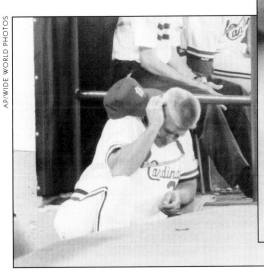

Two managers who did not last through the 1990 season, Bucky Dent (right) and Whitey Herzog (left). Dent was fired by George Steinbrenner, but Herzog quit after ten years in St. Louis. "I just couldn't get them to play," he said.

Take it from Sparky Anderson:(above) "You don't have to be a Harvard professor to be a manager."

Eric Gregg gives Tommy Lasorda the old heave-ho.

After their celebrated joint holdout, Sandy Koufax and Don Drysdale finally came to terms with GM Buzzie Bavasi and the Dodgers in 1965. TV star Chuck Connors served as a middleman.

Mickey Mantle, shown here with Yankee President Dan Topping, wasn't all smiles during the '50s when he had to negotiate his salary.

As a GM Harry Dalton was on the receiving end of two of baseball's most lopsided trades, acquiring Frank Robinson for the Orioles and Nolan Ryan for the Angels.

Phil Rizzuto and Allie Reynolds casually study the fine print of their contracts as GM George Weiss looks on.

After Frank Robinson was traded from the Reds to the Orioles for pitcher Milt Pappas, Baltimore won four pennants in the next six years. The Cubs dealt Lou Brock to the Cardinals for pitcher Ernie Broglio. When Broglio pitched, Cub fans used to chant, "Where's Brock?"

The Kansas City Athletics traded Roger Maris to the Yankees after the 1959 season. He is shown here in 1958 (above) and in 1961 (below) after his record-breaking sixty-first homer.

Nolan Ryan throwing the first of his record six no-hitters. At the plate for K.C. is Amos Otis, who was also unwisely traded from the Mets.

does good chemistry win games, or does winning create good chemistry? Of course they feed off each other, which is Darling's point. "Winning initially creates good chemistry," he said, "and then as the season progresses, good chemistry *sustains* winning. Everybody's gung-ho in the spring. Chemistry comes to the fore in the dog days, when guys have to bring it up a notch."

As it turned out, Darling was no longer around for the Mets' dog days, as he was dealt to the Expos for reliever Tim Burke shortly after the All-Star break. At that point the Mets still hoped to make a run at the first-place Pirates, when their season disintegrated in anger, embarrassment, and frustration.

When Vince Coleman returned from a lengthy stay on the disabled list, he shouted a stream of invective at coach Mike Cubbage over a misunderstanding as to when he was scheduled to take batting practice. The increasingly ineffectual Harrelson declined to discipline Coleman. "What if I asked him to apologize and he said 'no'?"

So thoroughly had Harrelson abdicated his managerial responsibilities that in a loss to the Cubs in New York he sent pitching coach Mel Stottlemyre out to make a pitching change because, by his own admission, he did not want to be booed by irate fans.

In a stretch beginning in late July, the Mets dropped seventeen of nineteen games, including eight in a row to the Cubs. They were all but eliminated from the pennant race at the earliest date since 1983. Flogging the players, the manager, and the front office became a late-summer pastime for the team's fans, and wholesale personnel changes were predicted for the off-season. "You can't even be polite and call it the downfall of a team," said the usually reticent McReynolds. "It's been a garbage dumping."

PART 4

THE GM'S

BURDEN

Ten Terrible Trades

Before the rise of the Players Association, even veteran ballplayers did not have the option to veto a trade. Their only response to the news was, as former Indians' reliever Jim Kern put it, "Oh, who to?" Courtesy and consultation seldom entered into the transaction. Bob Uecker jokes about one of the times he was traded: "The manager just informed me, man to man—'No visitors allowed in the clubhouse.'"

In the good old days general managers traded with impunity; nothing stood in their way. All it took was a phone call. That's how Cleveland's consummate trader Frank Lane engineered a swap in 1960 of home-run leader Rocky Colavito for Detroit's batting champion Harvey Kuenn.

Of course, the other side of the coin for the GM was the possibility of living forever in baseball infamy as the architect of one of the most senseless, team-damaging deals of all time. In the last thirty years, there have been some real doozies. Here is an informal ranking of the Top Ten Best/Worst Trades, and the stories behind them:

1. FRANK ROBINSON FOR MILT PAPPAS   December 9, 1965

Bill DeWitt of the Cincinnati Reds sent an "old" Frank Robinson, at age thirty, to the Baltimore Orioles for Milt Pappas. The Orioles, in a generous mood, even threw in pitchers Jack Baldschun and Dick Simpson. DeWitt was operating by the dictum that it was better to trade a player a year too early rather than a year too late. Still, it was the ultimate insult to a player of Robinson's stature, and he reacted to it the way he reacted to pitchers brushing him back or hitting him with pitches. He made them pay for it on the field with home runs and game-winning plays.

The trade was finalized in December 1965. Lee MacPhail was leaving the Orioles to work for the Commissioner's Office, so the new general manager, Harry Dalton, was asked to approve the trade. "Lee did all the spade work on it," said Dalton. "It just came to a head as we made the administrative change. All I had to do was review it and give it my okay, which I did of course. I held it up for twenty-four hours because I tried to get another left-handed pitcher thrown in from Cincinnati, but I couldn't do it. After twenty-four hours, I figured, I'm not going to kill this, but Lee was worried on the sidelines that I was going to blow it by trying to get too much."

The reaction to the trade was immediate. Gene Woodling, then a Baltimore coach, said, "If we don't win the pennant this year with him, then we all ought to be fired. He'll be the best hitter the Orioles ever had."

In his first year with Baltimore, Frank Robinson dominated the American League. He hit forty-nine homers and won two games with homers in the four-game World Series sweep over the Dodgers. He won the American League MVP award and the World Series MVP award.

Robinson opened a new era in the American League, turning the Orioles from a contending team to one that went to the World Series four out of six years, missing only in '67 and '68. Before he was done, Robinson would hit 586 homers in his career. Milt Pappas, for his part, posted years of 12–11 and 16–13 for the Reds, then moved on to the Braves and then the Cubs. He won a total of ninety-nine games in the National League, including a no-hitter against the Padres. The Cincinnati fans and press understood that everybody makes mistakes, and decided to let bygones be bygones, as long as they could tie DeWitt to the bumper of a pickup truck and drag him around the city square for a few hours.

2. LOU BROCK FOR ERNIE BROGLIO   June 15, 1964

Brock was signed for a bonus by the Chicago Cubs out of Southern University in Baton Rouge, Louisiana. In his first professional season in 1961 he did it all in the Northern League, hitting .361 and stealing thirty-seven bases. He was only twenty-two years old when he was called up to the Cubs and over two full seasons and part of a third, he was zinged with the label of "butcher" for his fielding lapses. "Brock," they jeered, as in "rock."

The Cubs needed pitching and were talking to the Cardinals about acquiring Ernie Broglio. He had won twenty-one games in 1960, nine in '61, twelve in '62, and eighteen in '63. He wasn't a favorite with management, however, because he lived in a shady section of St. Louis called Gaslight Square where there was plenty to do at all hours of the night. Broglio liked to party and wouldn't move even after the front office strongly suggested he relocate to a more upscale area.

Just before the trading deadline the Cardinals were on the team bus heading for the Los Angeles airport for a midnight flight to Houston. The Dodgers had just beaten the Cardinals, and general manager Bing Devine slid into the seat next to manager Johnny Keane. "I can make that deal with the Cubs for Brock," he said, "but they will want Broglio." Nearly comatose after a tough loss, Keane looked straight ahead, never changing his expression. "Make it!" he said.

The trade sent Brock with pitchers Jack Spring and Paul Toth to the Cards for Broglio, veteran pitcher Bobby Shantz, and outfielder Doug Clemens. The Cardinals hadn't wanted Brock for his fielding. He didn't have an especially good arm, so they put him in left field instead of right. They took him for his hitting potential, and his blazing speed.

Brock hit .348 over his first 103 games with the Redbirds and stole thirty-three bases. He was a key as the Cards won the '64 pennant the last day of the season. He hit .300 in the '64 Series. He was just warming up for future Fall Classics. In 1967, against the Red Sox, he hit .414 and stole seven bases. In the '68 Series he hit .464 with seven more stolen bases. He finished with an incredible .391 average in three Series, making him, along with Reggie Jackson and a few others, one of the great World Series hitters of his time.

Brock stole fifty or more bases for ten straight seasons. In the year he broke the stolen base record with 118 steals, he stole fifteen bases against the Cubs without being thrown out, and five of his last seven steals were against the Cubbies. He tormented the National League catchers for nineteen years, had 3,023 hits, hit .297 for the Cardinals over his career, and breezed into the Hall of Fame.

Broglio's career went the other way. Perhaps in overthrowing to prove his own worth, he soon lost his fastball. In 1964 he was 7–12. Whenever Broglio pitched, Cub fans, not known for their charitable nature, chanted "Where's Brock? Where's Brock?" In 1965 Broglio developed bone chips, went 1–6, and the next year he was 2–6 with an ERA near 7.0. He flopped around in the minors and then retired in a literal blaze of glory. He put his jockstrap, uniform, socks, shoes, hat, and glove on his front lawn and lit a career-ending bonfire.

3. NOLAN RYAN FOR JIM FREGOSI   December 10, 1971

After the 1971 winter meetings, the Mets were the only team in the majors that hadn't made a trade. The hyperactive New York press ripped the front office pretty good, and chairman of the board Donald Grant was screaming for the organization to do something, *anything.* They did something all right. They sent Nolan Ryan to the California Angels.

Harry Dalton, the man who finalized the Frank Robinson deal, was now looking to rebuild his new team, the California Angels; he wanted to land a few young players for one established veteran. His most marketable product was 1971 All-Star shortstop Jim Fregosi. He was now playing third base for the Angels and the Mets needed a third baseman. The Angels had Ken McMullen to play third and they had acquired shortstop Leo Cardenas for pitcher Dave LaRoche, so they felt secure in trading Fregosi. As it turned out, Cardenas was a bust, but while they held him Dalton felt free to shop around for the best Fregosi offer. He craved a pitcher and the Mets had them in abundance—Seaver, Jerry Koosman, Gary Gentry, Jim McAndrew, and Nolan Ryan. Dalton did it this way—he asked for Gentry. Met general manager Bob Scheffing recoiled at this opening gambit, so Dalton quickly injected Ryan's name into the conversation.

"I wanted Ryan because I knew he wasn't likely to be a starter with the Mets," Dalton recalled. "We knew he threw as hard as anybody in baseball, but, unfortunately, nobody knew whether it was going to be a ball or a strike." Ryan was the fifth starter at the time for the Mets, frequently dropped from the rotation for off-days and rainouts. In 1971, Ryan had begun with a 7–2 record, but faltered in the second half, wound up completing only three of twenty-six starts, and had a 10–14 record and a 3.97 ERA.

Whitey Herzog was then the director of player development for the Mets. Looking back, he said, "We had other starters who threw darn near as hard as Nollie, but they were pitchers and he was still a thrower. He couldn't get his curve over, and he had yet to develop a change-up. I told Harry, 'He'll fill your park if you get him' but I honestly didn't think the Mets would trade Ryan."

Scheffing called Herzog on a Saturday night, and said, "Would you get hold of Leroy Stanton [an outfielder] and tell him we just traded him for Fregosi?"

Herzog told him he wouldn't trade Stanton for Fregosi. "I just saw Fregosi play." When Herzog picked up the Sunday paper, he saw that the Mets indeed had gotten Fregosi, and given up Ryan, Stanton, and two other players, Don Rose and Francisco Estrada.

Fregosi, then the forty-sixth man to play third base for the Mets, was, like all the others before him, a near-complete washout. The first ball hit to him in a spring training game went between his legs, and the next day he broke his finger. By the time he got into the lineup, he was overweight and out of shape, and hit only .232 for the Mets. A year later he was sold to the Rangers.

Ryan, meanwhile, was winning nineteen games in 1972 and leading the AL with 329 strikeouts. He was into his Hall of Fame groove.

4. NORM CASH FOR STEVE DEMETER   April 12, 1960

When Frank Lane of the Indians called the Tigers in 1960 to offer Cash for Demeter, the Tiger GM Rick Ferrell was momentarily con-

fused. "You mean cold cash or Norm Cash?" It was five days before
Frank sent Rocky Colavito to the Tigers for Harvey Kuenn. "Trader
Frank" was certainly not afraid to roll the dice that year.

Lane had only just received Norm Cash in a multi-player deal with
the Chicago White Sox, and, true to his revolving-door policy,
shipped him out before he could ever play with the Indians. Cash hit
eighteen homers for the Tigers in 1960, and then, as a full-time player
in 1961, hit .361 with forty-one homers and 132 RBIs, one of the
great years of the whole postwar era. Before he was through, he hit
374 homers.

The estimable worth of Steve Demeter to the Indians? He batted
five times in 1960 and didn't get a hit, and that was the end of a big-
league career that spanned twenty-three at-bats.

5. STEVE CARLTON FOR RICK WISE   February 25, 1972

In 1971 Steve Carlton reached the plateau that pitchers dream
about—a twenty-win season. In the last years before free agency,
Carlton went to Cardinals owner August Busch, Jr., and requested
a raise. If he didn't get it, he was going to hold out. Busch was going
to teach him a lesson, and set an example for any other ballplayer
who wanted to be paid what he thought he was worth.

Carlton was traded/exiled to the last-place Phillies for starting
pitcher Rick Wise, who had won seventeen games for the lowly Phils.
Wise, who had pitched for the Red Sox in the American League, was
nothing special in St. Louis, recording a 33–28 record with the Cardinals. In 1972 Carlton had perfected a biting slider, paired with a
sweeping curve and a high fastball. He had one of the greatest single-
season pitching performances in history. He won twenty-seven games
for a team that finished dead last, with a 1.97 ERA, and he struck
out 310 batters.

Carlton was an original. He trained by pulling his arm through vats
of rice and working it to the bottom of a bucket of sand. He set new
standards for public relations by refusing to talk to the press for most
of his career. He pitched with cotton in his ears to shut out crowd
noise as well as his teammates. But whatever he did worked for him.

Eventually, with the help of Mike Schmidt, he turned the Phillies around and led them to five division titles and a world championship in 1980, winning the seventh game of the World Series.

6. GEORGE FOSTER FOR FRANK DUFFY AND VERN GEISHERT

May 29, 1971

San Francisco Giants president Horace Stoneham had a surplus of outfielders going into the 1971 season. Willie Mays still played center, Bobby Bonds was in right, and Ken Henderson was the left-fielder. George Foster wasn't showing the Giants very much, so it was hardly a gut-wrenching decision to trade him to the Reds for some infield help and a young pitcher.

The Reds showed a lot of patience with the sometimes aloof outfielder. In fact, it was another several years before Foster found his power stroke, but when he did the numbers he put up were stupendous. He hit twenty-three home runs in 1975 and twenty-nine in 1976, and then became the tenth player ever to crack the fifty-homer barrier in 1977 when he hit fifty-two with 149 runs batted in. Foster became the first to hit fifty since Maris and Mantle both did it in 1961, and it was another thirteen years before Cecil Fielder joined that select club.

Foster's accomplishment is even more imposing when considering how many Hall of Fame sluggers never hit fifty homers, including Hank Aaron, Lou Gehrig, Harmon Killebrew, and Willie McCovey. After all, only four players in the history of the game ever hit fifty homers twice in their careers—Ruth, Kiner, Mantle, and Foxx.

Foster led the league three times in RBIs, twice in home runs, hit over .300 four times, and wound up with 348 career home runs, all but four coming after he left the Giants. Foster thus joined an illustrious list of sluggers who were peddled by the Giants, including Orlando Cepeda, Bobby Bonds, Dave Kingman, Darrell Evans, and Jack Clark.

Frank Duffy spent a year with the Giants playing shortstop and batted .179 before he was shipped to Cleveland. The Reds had also thrown in Vern Geishert, who had won only one game in the big leagues prior to the trade, and didn't even make the Giant ballclub. Nobody remembers Vern, but nostalgia isn't what it used to be, is it?

7. ROGER MARIS COMES TO THE YANKEES December 11, 1959

In the early years of the Kansas City Athletics, they served as a farm team for the New York Yankees, giving up their best players in lopsided trades. From the A's the Yankees acquired players like Clete Boyer, Ryne Duren, and Bobby Shantz, Art Ditmar, Bob Cerv, Bud Daley, and Hector Lopez. In thirteen years, Kansas City traded with the Yankees sixteen times, involving fifty-nine players. They never got the best of the trade.

Players went back and forth in this charade as on a shuttle. If a young player faltered in New York, like pitcher Ralph Terry, he went to K.C. to get his act together, and returned to the Yankees after he was straightened out. (In that deal, Billy Martin accompanied Terry to K.C. as punishment for Martin's birthday celebration with teammates at the Copacabana that wound up as a headline-making brawl.) And if the Yankees thought an older player might be over the hill, like Enos Slaughter, they let him prove he still had what it takes in Kansas City, and *then* brought him back for the pennant race.

This incestuous relationship was presided over by the first owner of the Athletics in Kansas City, Arnold Johnson, who was a business associate and close friend of the co-owner of the Yankees, Del Webb. While their "arrangement" was in effect, the greatest player that the Athletics sent to the Yankees was Roger Maris. Maris was traded along with shortstop Joe DeMaestri and first baseman Kent Hadly. K.C. got Hank Bauer, Don Larsen, Norm Siebern, and Marvelous Marv Throneberry. Bauer and Larsen were over the hill, but Siebern gave the A's some good years, so this trade may not be one of the truly worst of all time, but the transaction involving the single-season home-run king stands symbolically for all the prime talent that Kansas City freely shipped to New York.

There had been hints of Maris's potential. One year he hit thirty-three homers in the minors. In 1959 he was leading the American League in batting average with a .344 mark as late as July 28, but then slumped to drop his season average down to .273. When he came to Yankee Stadium, he worked on pulling the ball to take advantage of the short right-field porch, and his classic stroke made him into a great power hitter. Many people think of Roger Maris as a one-year wonder, but he won the MVP award in 1960 with thirty-nine homers, before he ever made the assault on Ruth's record.

He won the MVP award again in 1961 with his record sixty-one homers. And he had another solid season in 1962, although his homers fell off to thirty-three. In 1963 he injured his hand, which made it hard for him to pull the ball with authority. The Yankees failed to tell him that X rays showed the hand was actually broken. The fans, many of whom had wanted Mantle to break Ruth's home-run record, booed the hell out of Maris once he became less productive. Still, with Maris playing right field and batting third, the Yankees went to the World Series five years in a row, 1960–64.

8. AMOS OTIS FOR JOE FOY   December 3, 1969

In 1969, two years before the Nolan Ryan deal, the Mets were trying to solve the Third Base Problem. Sound familiar? Joe Foy, formerly of the Red Sox, had hit .262 for Kansas City, and the Mets were hot for him since he had some power. So they gave up young Amos Otis and Bob Johnson for Foy. He quickly proved that he really couldn't hit or field anymore; his career as a regular was over within a year.

The Mets had tried to make Otis a third baseman, but the Royals were smart enough to turn him loose in center field, where he became a star, if not a superstar. Throughout the '70s, based on a full 162-game season, Otis *averaged* eighteen homers a year, a .284 average, and thirty-three stolen bases, which is, as they say, not too shabby. In fact, there wasn't a better center fielder in baseball for that decade. So the Mets not only failed to solve the Third Base Problem, but losing Otis gave them a new void in center field over the next decade, which was capably filled for only a few seasons by Tommie Agee.

9. RYNE SANDBERG AND LARRY BOWA   January 27, 1982
FOR IVAN DE JESUS

Dallas Green had just come over from the Phillies to be the general manager of the Cubs, and he knew Philadelphia's minor league system and the players in it. This enabled him to pull off a major steal. He dangled Ivan De Jesus in front of the Phillies, who gave him Larry Bowa and the young Ryne Sandberg. The Phillies figured Bowa was over the hill but two years after the deal Bowa helped the Cubs win the East. And by the way, Sandberg was the National League MVP that 1984 season.

The good news for the Cubs was that Sandberg got better even after having his "career year" in '84. His 1990 season was one of the greatest ever. Only two other players ever batted .300, hit forty homers, knocked in one hundred runs, and stole twenty-five bases in a single year: José Canseco in 1988 and Hank Aaron in 1963. Sandberg also holds the all-time career fielding percentage record for second basemen.

10. WILLIE MCGEE FOR BOB SYKES   October 21, 1981

Before the era of Steinbrenner's "baseball people," the hazy conglomeration of advisers who were held responsible for the woeful Yankee trades of the '80s, there was a single man responsible for the decisions—Gabe Paul. Paul had made some good deals for the Yankees—Bobby Bonds for Ed Figueroa and Mickey Rivers; Doc Medich for Willie Randolph, Dock Ellis, and Ken Brett—and was a prime architect of a championship team.

In the free-agent-happy mind of George Steinbrenner, nurturing young minor league talent and developing players in the majors was not the way to do it. The Yankees let pitching prospects like Cy Young winner Doug Drabek, World Series MVP José Rijo, Tim Belcher, and Jim Deshaies get away, and they lost genuine power hitter Fred McGriff in a minor trade. Among the young prospects that escaped them was a center fielder by the name of Willie McGee.

McGee had hit .322 in Double-A ball in 1981, but the Yankees decided he wasn't their center fielder of the future. The Yankees were not even going to keep McGee on their forty-man roster, so were almost certain to lose him in the minor league draft. Yankee general manager Bill Bergesch offered McGee to the Cardinals and asked for pitcher Bob Sykes in return.

Sykes started the next season in Triple-A and worked his way down to Double-A. McGee, in his first year with St. Louis, hit .296, played great center field, and in the World Series had a memorable game against the Brewers when he hit two homers and made two fabulous catches against the fence.

Steinbrenner was so incensed at being taken that he demanded additional compensation for McGee from Augie Busch. He got it. The politics behind the scenes was that Busch wanted to get rid of commissioner Bowie Kuhn, and Steinbrenner threatened to vote for Kuhn's retention if Busch didn't come up with some players. And so Busch sent Stan Javier and Bobby Meacham to the Yankees. That helped some but didn't come close to evening things out, especially after McGee won the MVP award in 1985.

Among the runner-up stinkers of the last thirty years there was the Mets trade of Jeff Reardon for oft-injured head-case Ellis Valentine; the Red Sox sending Sparky Lyle to the Yankees in return for Danny Cater; the Orioles burning the Yankees in a multi-player deal, acquiring Tippy Martinez, Rick Dempsey, and Scott McGregor for Rudy May and Ken Holtzman; and the Dodgers picking up Pedro Guerrero from the Cleveland Indians for pitcher Bruce Ellingsen, who won the grand total of one game in the big show.

The Braves got the butt end of one of the worst deals when they sent Brett Butler and third baseman Brook Jacoby to Cleveland for pitcher Len Barker in 1984. Barker fell flat on his mustache, bringing up the question of how an Atlanta franchise could ever trade a guy named *Brett Butler* in the first place.

Gimme That Old-Time Negotiating

In the age of arbitration, where a player can seek a fair settlement of his contract, baseball executives are having a hard time adjusting to the astronomical new salaries, some of which resemble the zip code of the planet Saturn. Ken "Hawk" Harrelson, former player, manager, general manager, and broadcaster, predicts that the '90s will see the first $10 million-per-year ballplayer, and that in twenty or thirty years, depending on baseball's future television contracts and the possibility of pay-per-view revenue, ballplayers could be making $50 million annually.

It's important to remember, however, what things were like before the courts changed the laws governing baseball in the mid-'70s. Before free agency, the general managers were the feudal lords of the game, and at contract time they greeted players as they would any groveling serf. Negotiating a player contract in baseball used to be a one-way street. The general manager would listen to a player's request and then cajole, hoodwink, or otherwise screw him with vim and vigor.

It was not just the run-of-the-mill player who got taken—the stars of the game were basically in the same position. After Joe DiMaggio hit safely in fifty-six games in 1941, setting the hitting record that may never be broken, Yankee GM Ed Barrow offered him a $2,500 pay cut. Barrow had a rule with the players. They were forbidden to talk with their teammates, and especially to the press, about their salaries. When DiMaggio talked about his dissatisfaction with the Yankee front office to the newspapers, Barrow reacted badly. He accused

DiMaggio of being greedy at a time when so many Americans were fighting a war at low pay themselves. DiMaggio discovered early on that getting money out of the Yankees was like pulling teeth, if you're talking about yanking molars bare-handed without an anesthetic.

When Mickey Mantle was a rookie he was signed for $7,500, only because Casey Stengel talked the Yankees into raising it from $5,000. The next year he hit .311 and got $10,000. The he went to $12,500, then $17,000. After establishing himself as one of the best players in baseball, he got a raise for the 1956 season to $32,500. And then he went out and had the greatest season of his life, winning the Triple Crown. He hit .356 with fifty-six homers.

The negotiations for the 1957 season were sure to be brutal. Mantle went in and asked to have his salary doubled to $65,000. General manager George Weiss told Mantle that he was making an impossible demand. But Mantle knew that Williams and Musial and Mays were all making around $100,000, and he had had a better year than any of them.

Weiss told Mickey, "You're twenty-five years old—a baby. How much will you want ten years from now if I keep doubling your salary?" Mantle wouldn't budge so Weiss took out a folder. "I wouldn't want this to get into Merlyn's [his wife's] hands. It could hurt your image, Mickey." Incredulous, flabbergasted, and ashamed, Mantle found himself looking at detective reports, such as: "*Mickey Mantle and Billy Martin left the St. Moritz Hotel at 6:00 P.M. Came in at 3:47 A.M.*" There were reams of typed pages, and photographs covering every move he had made off the playing field.

It soon became apparent that the Yankees were not necessarily looking after Mantle for his own good, or even to protect their investment in him, but more for the sake of gaining leverage in a contract negotiation. Weiss may not have wanted to resort to this ploy, but he obviously felt he had no recourse but to pull out all the stops, even if they were morally or legally shady.

Mantle told Weiss he wouldn't play—he'd stay home and run his bowling alley in Dallas and his motel in Joplin, Missouri. Go ahead, said Weiss, stay there in Dallas. As Mantle walked out of the office, ready to be sick to his stomach, Weiss told him that he might very well trade him to the Indians for Rocky Colavito and Herb Score.

So Mantle sat around his house—tense, depressed, and buried in despair. Then Yankee president Del Webb called and convinced him to come down to spring training in St. Petersburg. Mantle presented his case to Webb, who shook his hand and had a contract drawn up for $65,000. Now that wasn't so hard, was it?

It was one of the few times that a Yankee got the better of George Weiss. Mantle went out in 1957 and, after hitting .365 with thirty-four homers, was feeling pretty good about his performance. Yet he had hit twenty-two homers less than in his 1956 Triple Crown year. So the Yankees wanted to cut his salary.

It had happened before. In 1950 Phil Rizzuto won the MVP when he hit .324 and came into Weiss's office wanting fifty grand for the following year. When backed against the wall, Weiss would resort to trickery. He gave him a contract for $35,000 and added $15,000 in a separate, personal check, "out of my own pocket." And then, the next year, when the Scooter went back to hitting his career average of .274, Weiss began negotiations with the starting point being Rizzuto's $35,000 contract, having conveniently forgotten all about that extra $15,000.

There was at least a grain of truth in Weiss telling a player that his salary was coming out of Weiss's own pocket. He had an arrangement with the Yankee top brass that he would get 10 percent of anything left over from the salary budget. (Later, pitcher Ed Lopat found out that Weiss was keeping a percentage of the leftover money for himself; he told the rest of the players, who were none too happy about it.)

To keep the budget down for his own profit, Weiss would haggle with players and reason with them using his own form of inimitable pretzel logic. He would try to convince Yankee ballplayers that they should accept less money in salary because they could practically depend on receiving a World Series share, which in those days was a good portion of a season's salary for most of the players. Of course, if the Yanks didn't win it all, Weiss would then attempt to cut salaries that didn't include the raise he failed to give them the year before because they had expected a World Series share.

Weiss and his assistant Roy Hamey worked a version of the old good cop/tough cop routine. In this time-honored police tactic, the first cop trying to get a confession out of a suspect will try to scare and threaten, and then the soft cop will come in, and with a gentler tone, advise the suspect to talk to him to avoid having to deal with that other lunatic. The Yankee players would have to deal with Roy Hamey first, and he was so insulting and hard-nosed that when Weiss offered the player just a little more, the player would be grateful.

Weiss operated the team like it was his family and he was the "godfather." If the wife or child of a player became ill, Weiss made sure the best doctors were available for them, and he would get them loans if they needed them, anything to foster this paternal relationship with players, who were in many respects treated like children.

The other truth about George Weiss was that he developed more good players from his farm system than anyone in baseball history. After the Yankee era waned in the mid-'60s, he went over to the Mets and nurtured pitchers like Seaver, Koosman, and Ryan, and put together the roots of what would be yet another championship team.

Also, Weiss wasn't an exception to the rule of the GM. Almost all of them in this age of baseball rooked the players any way they could. Consider how another legendary baseball franchise, the St. Louis Cardinals, dealt with the two greatest pitchers in their history at salary time.

When Dizzy Dean won thirty games in 1934, and two more in the World Series against Detroit, he got a raise to $18,500. The next year he won twenty-eight and was going to ask for $50,000 but Branch Rickey cut him down to $17,500 because he'd won two less games. Rickey, according to Enos Slaughter, "would go into the vault for a nickel."

Things hadn't changed much with the Cardinals thirty years later. Bob Gibson won nineteen games in 1964, then twenty in 1965, but GM Bob Howsam offered a $2,000 raise instead of the $15,000 raise that Gibson wanted because after all, he'd won only one more game. It was outrageous, of course, but typical.

Even in the '60s, the ballplayer waited at home for the club to send him the coming season's contract offer, always looking forward to it with mixed emotions. On the one hand the player felt the anticipation of opening a present on Christmas morning. On the other he knew in his bones it was going to be the equivalent of the gift that nobody wants, the rock-hard fruitcake, the loud tie, the proverbial rotting fish, an offer so low that the player was going to have to send it back posthaste.

In 1969 pitcher Stan Williams was not pleased when he received his contract in the mail from the Indians' general manager Gabe Paul. First, a little background: Williams was a tough pitcher who developed arm trouble. It was the only bad arm that he had in his career, but unfortunately it lasted for six and a half years. He was out of the major leagues for three years, and reached the bottom when he found himself in Triple-A ball giving himself one last chance to make it back in 1967. "I would throw a sixty-eight-mph fastball and just cry," he said, "but it was my only way of getting an income, so I stayed with it."

Then one day he was backing up one of the pitchers in pregame drills and somebody asked for a ball and he threw it and something just popped on the top of his right shoulder. Later, warming up in the bullpen that day, his ball was moving real well, and his arm didn't hurt, and Williams was called into the game and struck out seven in three innings. His arm was back, and he was called up to the big leagues a month later by Indians manager Joe Adcock. He pitched well at the end of the '67 season, but Gabe Paul didn't want to give him what he wanted, $27,500 for the next year. Despite having pitched in winter ball as well, Paul said he hadn't yet proved that his arm was sound. Gabe offered $11,000, take it or leave it. Williams took it.

So Williams went out in 1968, and won thirteen games with a 2.50 ERA, and then waited for his contract to arrive, hoping just to get back to what he was making before he had the arm trouble. "Gabe sent me the same contract again, and I kicked the bathroom door off the hinges, and sat down and wrote a letter. My asking price had gone from $30,000 to $35,000, for pissing me off, and I also wanted to be reimbursed for two suitcases I lost in Portland in Double-A that I was never paid for, and I threw in the price of the bathroom door. And then I wrote, 'Don't write and don't call me unless you agree to my terms. No bartering.' "

Gabe called Williams and said, "Stan, Stan, I just sent that contract out to beat the deadline. I'd have torn it up if you'd signed it. There's no problem, Stan, you'll get what you wanted." "Yeah," Williams said, "Gabe would have torn it up. That would be the day."

Any prominent general manager worth his membership in this peculiar fraternity developed some creative tricks for holding down player salaries. Buzzie Bavasi, longtime GM for the Dodgers, was right at the head of the class.

"One year," recalled Bavasi, "I had signed Tommy Davis to a contract for $50,000. Ron Fairly was coming in to negotiate his contract, and I knew he was going to ask for far more than I felt he was worth. So I had a dummy contract drawn up. It showed that Tommy Davis would be paid $18,500. I put it on my desk, where it could be seen easily.

"When Fairly came into the office, I came up with an excuse to leave for a minute. I knew Fairly would peek at the dummy contract. When he saw that Davis would make only $18,500, he figured he could not ask for more money than a National League batting champion was getting. Fairly signed for $18,500."

Before the 1966 season, Bavasi was using another tactic to hold down the salaries of his two star pitchers, Sandy Koufax and Don Drysdale. He was telling Drysdale he couldn't give him what Koufax was getting, and telling Koufax that he couldn't make that much more than Drysdale. When the pitchers talked about what was happening in their negotiations, they decided to make an end-run around Buzzie by holding out together. They would negotiate the same points and the same amount of money—three-year contracts for $500,000 each.

No one in baseball had a multi-year contract at that time and owner Walter O'Malley would have none of it. In 1965 Koufax had made $85,000 and Drysdale had made $80,000. Bavasi's budget called for Koufax to be raised to $100,000 and Drysdale to be raised to $90,000. At their next meeting they said they'd settle for $150,000 a year for three years.

Bavasi said he could only give them $195,000 between the two of them, and they held out. Every day in Los Angeles the holdout was making headlines. At one point the dynamic duo threatened to go to Japan to pitch. Bavasi thought that was funny because baseball still had its reserve clause, and the Japanese leagues honored it.

Two weeks before the season opener, Chuck Connors, a former ballplayer and now a TV star, and a middle man for the two pitchers, called and told Bavasi that they were ready to sign. Bavasi, who was close to Connors, agreed to a meeting. The two came in and said they would settle for less than 150 grand each. The contracts were signed—$125,000 for Koufax, and $110,000 for Drysdale. (The holdout, incidentally, enabled a rookie pitcher named Don Sutton to make the team. He wound up winning twelve games that year en route to a 300-win career.)

Their ploy had worked, insofar as Koufax got a $40,000 raise and Drysdale a $30,000 raise. Unknowingly, however, they took money out of the pockets of the twenty-three other players. The Dodgers had budgeted $100,000 for salary increases for the entire ball club. When the two star pitchers took $70,000 of it, it left only $30,000 in raises for the rest of the team, and that's all they got.

Koufax had one of his greatest years in 1966. He won twenty-seven games, and then chose to retire. Drysdale won thirteen and lost sixteen, and pitched for three more years, losing as many games as he won. The significance of this dual holdout was that it portended far-reaching changes in the legal arrangements of the game. Players would not overturn the reserve clause and procure their rights as free agents until the '70s, but it was definitely blowin' in the wind around the time of the Dodger holdout.

In the mid-'60s, the players could not make any demands, and so they begged and pleaded that the minimum salary be raised from $7,000 to $10,000 per year. The owners wouldn't budge. As a result the players eventually hired a lawyer named Marvin Miller, who educated the players and taught them how to stand together.

"The irony of the whole thing," said Jim Bouton, "is that if the owners had said to us back in 1965, 'Not only will we raise the minimum salary from $7,000 to $10,000, but we'll raise the minimum $1,000 per year for the next twenty years,' we would have been happy with $11,000, $12,000, $13,000, we would have thought we were the richest guys in the world. But because they were so greedy, so inflexible, so rigid, they cost themselves millions and millions of dollars."

In 1976 baseball salaries made a quantum leap when owner Charles Finley reneged on paying for an annuity, and an arbitrator ruled that Catfish Hunter's Oakland contract was null and void, and Hunter was declared a free agent. Hunter had led the American League in 1975 with twenty-five wins and a 2.49 ERA. He signed a five-year contract with the Yankees for $3.75 million, at a time when the average annual major league salary was still $45,000. Other landmarks followed in the next decade: Nolan Ryan became the first $1 million-per-year player, and Pete Rose the first to make $2 million for a single season.

By the 1990 season, ten premier players were making $3 million per season on multi-year contracts; consistent regulars, good players if not real stars, were routinely being paid close to $2 million, and $1 million was being doled out to a lot of journeyman players. In 1991 Roger Clemens became the first player to make $5 million per year.

Jim Bouton questioned the fans and owners who now claimed the players were being overpaid. "What does it mean, 'being over-paid'?" he asked. "You are paid what somebody else thinks you are worth, nothing more, nothing less. If somebody pays you money, and you weren't as good as that person thought you would be, you were overpaid—and if you were better than they thought you would be, you were underpaid. But at any given moment in time, you were getting paid what an independent party thought you were worth."

Bouton also doesn't buy the notion that players do not perform at their highest level when they receive guaranteed multi-year contracts. "Businessmen don't believe it about themselves. No other profession believes that. Why do we believe it about athletes, especially when they got to the majors because they were the most competitive Little Leaguers, the most competitive players in high school, college, and the minors?"

If there is a decline in performance from getting a big contract, it may be due to the very opposite of not being hungry or a general loss of intensity—it may be because a player is *trying too hard* to justify a fat contract, and gets hurt as a result of trying to do too much. Andy Van Slyke, known as an ultimate hustler who loves the game so much he would play for nothing, signed a major three-year deal before the 1989 season, and fought nagging injuries the whole year, pulling a rib cage muscle from diving flat-out in center field. Later in the year he had a shoulder injury, fluid in his knees, and a pulled thigh muscle. He played on.

In any given year, some players will have good years, others will have average years, and some will have mediocre years, but only a few ballplayers will admit that money enters into the equation. Keith Hernandez is one. "When you're playing in the third year of a five-year contract," he said, "it's pretty hard to get up for the really tough pitchers." For that reason he preferred the three-year deal, where the money incentive was always around the corner.

If a previous generation of major league ballplayers had as their ultimate goal the Hall of Fame, perhaps the ultimate for many contemporary players has become the multi-year deal. The players for whom real money pressure hinges on virtually every pitch are the younger players, who have to establish themselves in their first three years so they can get to arbitration. If some think that money is not a prime game within the game, the kind of incentive that can produce winning baseball, they should check out what kinds of numbers players put up when their contracts are running out.

Baseball's New Hotseat

They used to say that major league managers are only "hired to be fired," but baseball has a new revolving door—for the people in the front office. More and more, the buck is stopping with the general manager, whose once-cushy position has become something of a hotseat.

The body count after the 1990 season included Larry Himes of the White Sox, fired because he couldn't get along with co-owner Jerry Reinsdorf and failed to acquire veterans for the pennant drive; "Trader Jack" McKeon of the Padres, who took the fall when new ownership was disappointed in the club's showing; and Bobby Cox of the Braves, who had his hands full managing a last-place team without the added weight of rebuilding the Atlanta franchise from the GM post.

Two other GMs left to join other organizations. John Schuerholz said good-bye to the Royals to run the Braves and Joe McIlvaine left the Mets and took the Padres job. Schuerholz was offered a much better contract, and McIlvaine was given the power he always wanted in New York. Both denied that their leaving had anything to do with their respective front offices having disappointing years.

It's open season on all general managers because they don't really work behind the scenes anymore. They're out there balancing on baseball's new high wire, their every move scrutinized by the media—including beat writers, national columnists, sports-talk radio hosts, and cable TV's baseball experts, among others. The armchair public is also more knowledgeable and watching closely. Fantasy baseball leagues, after all, are not really about being an owner or manager but a fantasy *general manager*.

Without question, the GM's job is more complex and more difficult than ever. Each day he must sift through box scores from all over the country, surveying the complete amateur baseball field from high school to college. He is the one who has to make crucial decisions on which young players have the tools, desire, and aptitude to make it to the majors.

General managers, with the help of their scouts, can rate players on their talent. There are all kinds of scientific ways to judge on-the-field performance. But what's inside the player? Aptitude tests are administered to prospects today to gauge their desire and intelligence, but the accuracy of such findings is suspect. (On one of these written tests, Milwaukee's future Hall of Famer Robin Yount got the lowest score ever.) After everything that can be objectively codified is added up, real insight into what makes a future major leaguer may come from gut instinct. Milwaukee Brewers GM Harry Dalton stressed that the very best indication he could get about a young player was from a scout that he could trust. " 'Either he can play,' he'll say, 'or he can't play.' "

It can be all-consuming for a general manager just to take care of what they call SDSD—Scouting, Drafting, Signing, and Developing. According to Dalton, the key to the job of general manager may be handling people—running a staff composed of a scouting director, a farm director, and his managers and coaches.

But once the season starts, the GM must also monitor the ongoing struggle of the major league team for possible weaknesses. One of the most important decisions he has to make is when to change managers, and then who to hire. Dalton is one of those GMs who has the power to make that determination himself. He made one of the most successful managerial switches in 1982 when he relieved Bob Rodgers and installed Harvey Kuenn as manager. "Harvey's Wall-bangers" went to the World Series.

"It was a veteran team," Dalton said of the switch, "that was ready to win. The total response of the club was not what it should be to Bob Rodgers. I felt Harvey was a knowledgeable baseball man and he was close to the players, they liked him. His approach was laid-back, and it fit that ball club. Harvey had veterans who knew how to play, and he let them."

Since baseball introduced divisional play in 1969, there have been twenty-nine teams with a losing record in the first half of the season whose general managers pink-slipped the manager. Only four of those teams finished above .500, and the 1982 Brewers were the only team to finish in first place.

"The most important thing in a manager," Dalton said, "is leadership. The manager's main job is to get the most out of the player for 162 games. Nobody does it perfectly, but the man who does it the best is going to win. If you told me you could have a so-so tactician and a great handler of men or vice versa, I'd take the people person every time."

In Dalton's opinion, the ideal manager, the one he would want on his side in a pennant race, was Earl Weaver. "He knew what his people could do, he knew what the opposition could do, and he was always a couple of innings ahead. He didn't have a doghouse; he could explode in a player's face and the next day not even remember it."

The most high-profile, if not the most important, job of the general manager is still the execution of trades. But there are contract restrictions on trading that make such transactions more difficult. Under today's rules, a player who has been in the majors for ten years and five with his current team can veto any trade. "Another factor besides the five-and-ten rule," said Dalton, "is that when the player has the right to say yes or no, then the agent comes into the picture, and the player is always looking for a financial inducement to accept an assignment, whether it's a bonus or an extra year on the contract. Then the sheer financial strength of the contracts can take a player out of another team's zone of interest right off the bat, because he's making too much money, or because the length of the contract is four or five years.

"So whereas twenty years ago, if you had a twenty-five man roster, you had maybe twenty tradable people, today you might have six or eight. And with twenty-six teams today, the talent is spread out more. Organizations just don't have the depth of talent in their minor league systems to help them put together a package of three or four players. Heck, in Baltimore in 1955, George Weiss and Paul Richards made a seventeen-player trade. Ten for seven! My goal all my life is to make one like that."

Since the advent of free agency in the early '70s, the focus of the general manager gradually shifted away from trading and to the available free agents. The bull market roared after the 1989 season; the number of ballplayers declaring free agency, around ninety, matched the previous high back in 1977. The bounteous crop of available players included such major talents as Mark Langston, who had led the American League in strikeouts on three separate occasions; Rickey Henderson, the all-time stolen base leader who had hit over .400 in the '89 playoffs and World Series; and National League Cy Young winner Mark Davis, who had forty-four saves. All were the kind of players who could push a contending team over the top, and everybody in baseball knew it.

Players of this stature expected to sign the richest contracts yet handed out by the baseball establishment. It was a far cry from a situation that existed after the 1986 season. Then a number of major players filed for free agency, but the owners appeared not to be interested in paying very much for the likes of Kirk Gibson, Jack Morris, Tim Raines, and others.

The courts later ruled that the owners had engaged in collusion when they failed to pursue the free agents, which was fairly obvious to the players at the time. André Dawson was a free agent in that off-season. He was desperate, because of his aching knees, to get out of Montreal and play the rest of his career in a home park with natural grass. Dawson eventually gave the Chicago Cubs a blank contract and actually told them to fill in the dollar amount. They filled in $500,000—a $700,000 cut in pay.

Dawson surprised the owners around the league by agreeing to the contract, figuring that he could have great years in Wrigley Field and make up the difference later on. "The Hawk" hit forty-nine home runs in his first year playing in Chicago, won the MVP award, got a raise, and never looked back.

After Orel Hershiser's dream season in 1988, which featured the record scoreless-inning skein and playoff and World Series heroics, he signed for $7.9 million over three years. He said that his contract would be a dinosaur in a year, and incredibly he was right. The new free agents who were premier or "franchise" players before the 1990 season were distinguished by their new market value of at least $3 million per year. "What you see," Hershiser said, referring to the new salaries, "is the $100 millon, $200 million the owners saved. Teams are not only competing for talent this year, but with the money they didn't use in the previous years."

It was a complex of factors that led to the skyrocketing salaries. One was the collusion, but the unprecedented free-spending atmosphere after the 1989 season also resulted from the new television contract. Major League Baseball's deal with CBS and ESPN gave each team $16 million per year for starters, and revenue from local TV and radio had skyrocketed for some teams. The Yankees, in particular, signed a twelve-year deal with the Madison Square Garden network for $500 million, or $45 million per year. When you throw in things like the luxury box craze that threw even more money in the owners' coffers, you have conditions so new and profitable for baseball that the issue of "fiscal sanity" had become, for the time being, largely irrelevant.

"There was a hysteria that took place," said Oakland GM Sandy Alderson. "It had a lot to do with the earthquake, which delayed the World Series ten days. That also delayed the free agent market ten days, just long enough to bring free agency to the winter meetings. When you get people together like that, it's like an auction, and you have impulsive buyers. It's like buying a *Star* at the checkout stand in the grocery store."

Baseball's traditional winter meetings were held that year in Nashville's Opryland Hotel, a sprawling edifice necessitating maps for discovering one's room. But the players' well-heeled agents had no trouble finding the money; all they had to do was sniff. Eyebrows were already raising in anticipation of the thawing of the collusion freeze-out when Kevin Bass and Nick Esasky each signed for over $5 million for three years. Both are considered good players, although nothing close to superstars.

The next major signing sent shock waves through baseball and let everyone know that the bidding wars had returned in earnest. Lanky sinker-baller Pascual Perez was a free agent, and the Expos wanted to re-sign him, so they offered $4 million for three years. George Steinbrenner entered the bidding and the Expos went up to $4.5 million, when Steinbrenner beat their offer by signing Perez to three years at $5.7 million.

General managers in both leagues scratched their heads and wondered why George would give Perez that contract, considering his background with drugs and alcohol, his hyperactive personality, and his 64–62 career record. When GMs factored in Perez being no youngster at thirty-two years of age, the consensus was that the flaky pitcher with the long greasy hair had pulled off one of the biggest heists in the history of the game. "I felt like regurgitating on myself," K.C. GM John Schuerholz said about the signing.

But nobody was more nonplussed than Charles Bronfman, the owner of the Expos. The Expos, after all, had taken Pascual off baseball's trash heap (he had been arrested for cocaine possession in the Dominican Republic in 1984) and given him the opportunity to redeem himself, which he had more or less. "I mean, you can have bidding for players," said Bronfman, "but you don't have to be a damn fool about it." By the end of December, he was openly discussing selling the franchise and "getting out of this damn business."

Free agents of all shapes and sizes, ages, and abilities were sucked up right and left, notwithstanding their deteriorating skills, substance-abuse problems, or poor performances. These signings and near-signings dominated the 1989 winter meetings and overshadowed all talk of trades. Teams were unsure of which deals to make without knowing where the free-agent chips would fall. And the negotiations with the agents were both time-consuming and draining for many of the GMs. As Montreal's Dave Dombrowski said, "You spend all your time talking to an agent, and you're mentally exhausted afterward. If you don't get him, you're frustrated on top of it and you have to regroup. Everybody kept saying they had to go back and regroup. I never heard that expression used as much as I heard it during the week. But it's true."

George Steinbrenner had fired the first volley in the new free-agent wars, and stood in front of an open vault of half a billion dollars in revenue from his cable TV deal, prepared to offer Mark Langston and Mark Davis the moon. Whatever offer they were able to get, he assured them of his ability to top it. In mid-November, the Mark Langston sweepstakes began in earnest, after Langston rejected a three-year, $10 million offer to re-sign with the Expos. Whitey Herzog flew out to meet Langston and talked up the great defense of his ball club and the dimensions of Busch Stadium. "If Mark pitched here," said Whitey, "he might never lose." The Dodger organization ushered Langston around Los Angeles. The Yankees and Angels got into it.

One of the many considerations that Langston had in choosing his venue was his wife Michelle's acting aspirations. Without regard to her thespian prowess, team representatives promised her that her career would prosper with them. Herzog told Langston his wife could appear with the St. Louis Municipal Opera and in a multitude of stage shows. Steinbrenner got Michelle a part in a soap opera taped in New York, but Angels owner Gene Autry one-upped him by arranging a role for her in *Airplane III*. It was the Angels who eventually signed Langston to a five-year deal for $14 million.

(The wives of the free agents were no small factor in some of the decisions. Pitcher Storm Davis was ready to sign with the Toronto Blue Jays when, on the same day, a crazed gunman murdered seventeen women in Montreal. Even though Montreal is 300 miles from Toronto, Davis's wife said no to Canada, and the pitcher signed with Kansas City.)

Mark Davis's agent tried for $16 million over five years after he had a $12 million offer from San Diego for four years, and the exasperated GM of the Padres, Jack McKeon, finally told Davis and his agent to take a hike. Davis had really wanted to stay in San Diego, and his wife termed the negotiating process at this point to be a "total nightmare." But he signed a four-year deal for $13 million with the Royals, so presumably Mrs. Davis no longer had to wake up screaming.

In bidding for both Langston and Davis, Steinbrenner was the clear-cut highest bidder, but was only being used to jack up the price. No one was interested in the Steinbrenner Yankees, an organization with no direction, a team with no stability, and with a lousy atmosphere to boot.

In the early days of free agency in the '70s, Steinbrenner was the first owner to realize what free-agent signings could do for a team. He dominated the market and won back-to-back world championships by signing Hall of Fame–caliber players like Catfish Hunter, Reggie Jackson, Goose Gossage, and later Dave Winfield. But those days were gone, and after ten years of treating his GMs and managers like puppets on strings, routinely criticizing players for choking, gutlessness, or spitting the bit, and centering the attention upon himself, Steinbrenner had fired or forced out so many good baseball people that the Yankee tradition was no more.

If GMs were unable to lure the blue-chip free agents, then they invariably went after whoever was available. Indians GM Hank Peters signed Keith Hernandez to a two-year deal for $3.5 million, bad legs and all. Even when Hernandez was still a very good player in the mid-'80s, he had to soak his aching pins in a hot tub after nearly every game. He was thirty-six, coming off a broken kneecap and several serious hamstring pulls, and the Indians brought him to a league where he didn't know the hitters or the pitchers. They also opened their checkbooks when the Rangers released journeyman pitcher Cecilio Guante. The Indians grabbed him at a bargain-basement price of $650,000.

Even teams that had long avoided the free-agent market, like the Detroit Tigers, plunged in with unprecedented zeal. The Tigers wound up signing Cecil Fielder, who had hit thirty-eight homers for the Hanshin Tigers in Japan. For $1.2 million, Fielder stunned the baseball world by hitting fifty-one homers, proving that there was indeed gold in them thar free-agent hills. But there were few Fielders out there, and in fact many of the big-name free agents such as Perez, Langston, and Mark Davis had unproductive seasons. And the Braves won the booby prize with their signing of Nick Esasky, who couldn't play at all in 1990 because of a $5 million case of vertigo and double vision that nobody could diagnose.

Baseball's salary structure had changed so rapidly that a payroll imbalance was created on many teams, and some players immediately wanted to renegotiate. Tony Gwynn suddenly became the low man on the San Diego Padres totem pole—the seventh-highest-paid player on the team going into the 1990 season; more than one hundred other players were making more than one of the game's very best hitters. "There are days when I wince when I read the sports pages," Gwynn said. "Believe me, no player is $2 million a year better than I am," he said bitterly. After his first full season in 1984 when he hit .351 and won his first batting title, he signed a six-year $4.6 million contract. After hitting .351 in 1987, he asked Padres president Chub Feeney for a two-year contract extension at $1.6 million per year.

"He laughed so hard he spit cigar ashes all over my face," Gwynn recalled. "There are some things you never forget, and I'll never forget that." When Dick Freeman moved in as the Padres president, he gave Gwynn a two-year extension in 1989 for $2 million per, but a year later that contract was hopelessly outdated as well. Gwynn finally caught up with the big boys in 1991 when his next multi-year contract paid him more than $4 million per season.

In the span of two years, team payrolls had grown from $10 million to $30 million for several teams. "I think it shocked everybody," said Dalton after the watershed winter of '89. "I don't think that people really expected it would happen, and I think that a lot of us are fearful as to what it's going to lead to. I think we all agree it's crazy, but it's a matter of whether you're going to protect your good talent and keep them on your club or are you going to lose them? Because we don't have a more favorable situation with supply and demand, we're all spending dollars we never expected to spend."

At the 1990 winter meetings, the signing that set the new trend in salary spirals was San Francisco GM Al Rosen's four-year, $10 million contract given to left-handed pitcher Bud Black (83–82 lifetime). There were the usual accusations of irresponsibility and insanity, but few teams held back from jumping in, including the Kansas City Royals. Even after being badly snake-bit with their free-agent signings of a year earlier, the Royals exhibited all the earmarks of an industry with money to burn, and landed pitcher Mike Boddicker from Boston with a hefty contract.

The teams were going ga-ga over the free agents because of the difficulty general managers have restructuring their ball clubs through trading. Of course, when a team dangles a valuable player as trade bait, everybody comes around. The major buzz of the 1989 winter meetings involved Cleveland Indians superstar Joe Carter, who had only one year left on his contract and wasn't going to re-sign with the Indians. Indians GM Hank Peters had no recourse but to trade him, so he sat back and listened to offers from virtually every major league team.

Trade rumors flew right and left. Peters heard from the Giants, the Red Sox, the Cards, the Rangers, the White Sox, and the Royals. Then San Diego's "Trader Jack" McKeon lit a cigar and went to work. McKeon had been holding his blue-chip catching prospect, Sandy Alomar, Jr., for just such a trade. He had tried to use Alomar and a pitcher to pry Ellis Burks from Boston, but after the Red Sox signed catcher Tony Pena, he set his sights on Carter. The Padres wound up throwing in streaky outfielder Chris James and a good minor league third-base prospect named Carlos Baerga, and a fair deal was finally struck.

It was a feather in the cap for both GMs, and a payoff for McKeon's patience in holding on to Alomar when he couldn't get what he wanted earlier. When Alomar, still playing behind Benito Santiago, had another banner season at the Triple-A level, his value went up and enabled the Padres to get a player that everybody wanted—Joe Carter.

Although Carter drove in 115 runs for the Padres in 1990, he only hit .232, and his leadership qualities were wasted on a team with so many warring factions. Following the season, the Padres completely gutted their baseball operation. The final body count was thirty-one firings in the front office, scouting department, and field positions, a search-and-sack mission that began with the dismissal of McKeon and the luring of Joe McIlvaine from the Mets to serve as the new GM.

McIlvaine took on the challenge of restructuring an underachieving team with gusto, and for the second year in a row the Padres were involved in the major trade of the winter meetings. McIlvaine sat down with Blue Jays GM Pat Gillick and proved there is no collective loss of nerve in their field by engineering what many have called "the deal of the century." Certainly there has never been a two-for-two trade of its kind involving young All-Star talent. San Diego sent Joe

Carter and second-baseman Roberto Alomar (still only twenty-two) to Toronto in exchange for first baseman Fred McGriff (thirty-five home runs, .300 average) and shortstop Tony Fernandez. It started with the two GMs throwing around some names and laughing about it, and ended with a good old-fashioned blockbuster.

Gillick had earned the nickname of "Stand Pat," because in the previous five years Toronto had made only one trade. That was before he decided to turn his team inside out. He signed left-handed setup man Ken Dayley as a free agent. Then he traded with the Angels for center fielder Devon White and pitcher Willie Fraser for outfielder Junior Felix and infielder Luis Sojo. After landing Joe Carter in the big deal with the Padres, left-fielder George Bell was allowed to exit via free agency. He would replace McGriff at first base with John Olerud, and try Manny Lee at shortstop in place of Fernandez. Gillick had reason to think he had improved the team's balance, speed, and leadership qualities. He wasn't through, either; during the 1991 season he traded several top prospects to secure the services of pitcher Tom Candiotti from the Indians.

But there have been recent teams that made even more drastic changes. The Jays, for instance, still have the same starting rotation. Revamping a team from top to bottom is still not impossible, at least not when the GM seat is occupied by Baltimore's Roland Hemond. He proved that baseball's executives are not totally helpless if they have to really clean house.

In the span of twenty-four months, Hemond completed nineteen trades. He signed Mickey Tettleton after his release from Oakland, acquired first baseman Randy Milligan and pitcher Dave Johnson for minor leaguers, and brought Phil Bradley back to the American League; he just never stopped dealing. He traded for more youth by moving high-priced veterans such as Eddie Murray, Fred Lynn, and Mike Boddicker. When the dust cleared, nineteen players on the 1989 forty-man roster were wearing a Baltimore uniform for the first time, and 170 of 186 nonbelieving baseball writers picked them to finish last. The last-place team that lost twenty-one games in a row in '88 became a fairy tale story the very next season, a ball club that was in the race to the last days, finishing second to Toronto.

Sometimes all you need is one move if it's the right one. After the 1988 season, GM Jim Frey had to take stock of the Chicago Cubs. The team had only won seventy-five games, but it was a deceiving number because they had blown twenty games out of the bullpen with the shell-shocked Calvin Schiraldi and aging Goose Gossage as their closers.

Frey felt he had to get somebody to anchor their bullpen and fearlessly traded a sweet-swinging, bonafide .300 left-hand batter, Rafael Palmeiro, to Texas for reliever Mitch Williams. Williams threw hard, but usually walked nearly a man per inning, was coming off arm trouble, and freely admitted his penchant for pitching as if his hair were on fire. A lot of fans, writers, and baseball people howled at this trade, but Frey was willing to take the heat, and Williams turned out to be the stopper who made it possible for the Cubs to win the pennant.

But, oh, what a difference a year makes. In 1990, Williams had more arm trouble and lost his fastball, while Palmeiro challenged for the AL batting title. It's the Rangers and GM Tom Grieve who are happy with the deal now, but they always were. To Frey's credit, he realized that Williams was the bullpen equivalent of Chinese food— a year later, the GM's hungry for a stopper again. So if there's a problem, throw money at it, which the Cubs did in signing closer Dave Smith, as well as two other major free agents, George Bell and Danny Jackson. And just before the 1991 season, Mitch Williams was traded to the Phillies.

Sandy Alderson of the Oakland A's may be the reigning King of the GMs. His acquisition of Willie McGee and Harold Baines for the 1990 stretch drive was just about unprecedented, and left a lot of his peers scratching their heads. But they already were. One of the reasons that this franchise went to the Series three years in a row is Alderson, working in perfect concert with his owner and manager.

In the spring of 1987, Alderson sent three minor leaguers to the Cubs for Dennis Eckersley, a starting pitcher that many, including Cub GM Dallas Green, thought had seen his best days. At the time the Eck was only several months out of rehab from his alcoholism, so he hadn't told the Cubs that he was clean and sober. The A's just liked his arm and knew he was a tremendous competitor, and by the following year he had become the premier closer in the game.

There have been a lot of great moves—signing Dave Henderson as a free agent, getting Bob Welch when they gave the Dodgers Jay Howell and Alfredo Griffin; you can go on and on. When a franchise is established as having a winning atmosphere, sometimes players will land in your lap, like possibly the greatest leadoff man in history, Rickey Henderson.

In the case of the A's, the rich get richer, and they have to be because the top players command the top dollar, and in that area the A's have made a concerted effort to keep their superstars happy. And yet there is trouble even in paradise. A year after Rickey Henderson signed a four-year contract for $12 million, he wanted to renegotiate the deal. Alderson's problem will be that of any contemporary GM—preventing his prime talent from bolting for greener pastures.

Even at the height of the A's dynastic years, Alderson continues to build with young players, having broken ground in awarding huge contracts to top prospects out of high school such as phenom pitcher Todd Van Poppel. He also signed college hurler Kirk Dressendorfer, so don't expect this club's starting rotation to shrivel up in the '90s just because of a postseason setback.

Which brings us to the Reds. It's really not too hard to see which GMs had the big years. Just look at who wins the World Series. Cincinnati had a lot of talent to begin with, but newly installed GM Bob Quinn, who had been excused from his duties by both the Indians and Yankees, had what you could call a "career year."

In the off-season he got Randy Myers for John Franco, basically an even trade, but it helped establish the Nasty Boy mystique in the bullpen. Quinn was with the Yankees in '89, and he knew how good the International League's batting champion Hal Morris was, and got him in a deal for pitcher Tim Leary. Lou Piniella liked this kid so much that if Piniella were still with the Yankees, he says he would put Don Mattingly in the outfield so that Morris could play first base! (Morris hit .340 for the Reds and is twenty-five years old.)

Right before the season, Quinn secured the services of World Series record-breaker Billy Hatcher from the Pirates for a minor league pitcher, which turned into a key move when Eric Davis went down. In mid-season he traded his extra starter, Ron Robinson, for Milwaukee's Glenn Braggs, who hit with authority and made a pennant-saving catch in the NLCS. The final big move down the stretch to assure that the Reds would go wire to wire was the acquisition of hometown boy Bill Doran from the Astros. Whatever the team needed, Quinn got it.

Of course, a GM like Quinn can lose his Midas touch just as quickly, which is the roller-coaster nature of the job. In June '91, one of the Reds' top prospects, first baseman Reggie Jefferson, was playing with Cincinnati when he came down with pneumonia. Instead of putting him on the disabled list, the Reds designated him for assignment back to the minors. But after ten days, Jefferson wasn't healthy enough to play anywhere; on a technicality, the team was going to lose him on waivers. So Quinn was forced to swallow hard and trade Jefferson to the Indians for a prospect who is probably three years away from being a major leaguer. For Quinn, reading Jefferson's name in the box scores will be tantamount to putting a little arsenic in his coffee every morning. The only consolation is that he's not alone, as last year Pirate GM Larry Doughty lost outfielder Wes Chamberlain, also his organization's number-one prospect, to the Phillies because of a similar snafu. Maybe these teams should invest in legal counselors to help interpret the new waiver rules.

The job of the general manager is a risky one. If he goes after a free agent, he's got to hope that the player will be productive, especially now that mediocre-to-good players command $2 million in salary. As Larry Himes said after he was fired by the White Sox, "The pressure the general manager feels from a large payroll is the resulting expectation of winning. If the players do not perform up to projected levels, the GM takes the heat for unwise investments."

Some of the GMs who have made the best moves over the last few years—such as Al Rosen of the Giants, Fred Claire of the Dodgers, and Sandy Alderson of the A's—also worked for ownership that had the finances to acquire major players. For teams like Montreal without the money, weather, or location to lure the big-time free agents, young and inexpensive players who can produce are far from a luxury but a matter of survival.

The best hedge against the inflating cost of fielding a competitive team is still a healthy farm system that churns out productive rookies. When the 1990 season started, the Expos had lost three-fifths of their starting rotation (Bryn Smith, Pascual Perez, and Mark Langston). In desperate-seeming moves, Montreal GM Dave Dombrowski signed Joaquin Andujar and Dennis Boyd, the latter having a terrific year while receiving injections to prevent clotting in his arm. But it was their young pitchers (Mark Gardner, Bill Sampen, Chris Nabholz, Brian Barnes, Mel Rojas, Steve Frey, and Howard Farmer) and exciting new position players like Delino DeShields, Marquis Grissom, and Larry Walker who made the team's future look very bright indeed.

Finally, having the best farm system alone generally will not be enough to win a championship, even if all the young players mature and peak within a year of each other. Today's GM must remain flexible and open to the possibilities of signing free agents and trading players, as well as drafting and developing prospects. Do something right in all three areas, and your team might still be playing when the leaves turn.

EPILOGUE

Fantasies for the Forgotten Fan

When the owners and players
clash over their collective bargaining agreements, and haggle over
dividing up baseball's monetary pie, all the fan can do is twiddle his
or her thumbs. The fan just doesn't figure into the equation. For
major league baseball is a monopoly that financially benefits only two
parties—the owners and the players.

The owners are not going to lock out the players in the future
because the Players Association wants cheaper tickets, lower prices
on the small Cokes at the concession stands, more parking at the
stadiums, or cleaner stadium toilets. The Players Association won't
insist that baseball not be televised via cable or pay-per-view so that
the economically under-privileged don't get shut out from watching
the games. Because while baseball players do indeed have a union,
they make up a special case as a group, very unlike coal miners in
West Virginia fighting for a meager living; you don't see ballplayers
marching in picket lines to support other unions.

By the same token, none of the owners will be trying to get the
players to cease and desist from charging little kids twenty bucks for
their autographs. There figures to be only one major point of contention between the rich owners and the rich players in the near
future and on into the brave new baseball world of the twenty-first
century—money, and lots of it.

But the fan, having no choice, has slowly become accustomed to
ballplayers making astronomical salaries. After all, the benefits ac-

cruing from the burgeoning popularity of the game should not be reaped strictly by ownership, and management would not be paying such salaries if they really could not afford it. The fan realizes as well that star ballplayers in this mediafied world have become, for better or worse, marketable entertainers as well as athletic heroes. Don't Hollywood actors make millions?

At the very least, the fan expects these players who make tens of thousands for every game to run out grounders all the way to first base and keep track of how many outs there are. For the most part, the fan does not begrudge players like Kirby Puckett or Dwight Gooden their money, not when he sees them exude such enthusiasm and intensity. What still rankles the fans, judging by two MVPs who got booed during spring training of 1991, are ballplayers whose egos will not allow them to appreciate their money and status. Rickey Henderson did not win any popularity contests for wanting to get out of his four-year $12 million contract just over a year after he signed it, and neither did Barry Bonds get much sympathy when he was so noticeably unhappy about losing in arbitration and having to accept $2.3 million for the season.

Still, those are true superstars. For some fans, watching mediocre players who earn over a million dollars per year to hit .220 is a pill as hard to swallow as the old horsehide itself, because the fan knows deep down that it is not just the owners who are footing the bill for the exorbitant salaries; it is baseball fans across the country. They pay for ballplayers' salaries not only by purchasing tickets to games, but when they pay for a sports cable channel or buy any of the products advertised at the stadium or on the radio and television broadcasts. Bad ballplayers who make a fortune can no longer be endearing for their miscues.

Opening Day is still one of the most magical days in sports, and once the first ball is thrown out, the fan soon hears the mitts a-poppin' and the bats a-crackin', and all is temporarily forgiven. But then, just when the vast legion of fans are being romanced again by the game that first seduced them in their youth, the baseball landscape is marred by some superstar's ongoing contract negotiation that can hog the headlines of the sports pages for the entire season. So even if they love the game more than they hate its big-business trappings, some fans have simply had it up to the brims of their thirty-dollar regulation Major League Baseball caps.

A small army of fans have already come up with a solution to their outcast status. Over a million of them have decided they would rather root for their own teams, and they now run their own franchises. They are Fantasy Owners obsessed with what some call the greatest game since baseball itself—Rotisserie Baseball, named after the restaurant where it was conceived.

Rotisserie is a simulation of a pennant race among ten teams composed of active major league baseball players who are drafted at a yearly auction. Cumulative team performances are tabulated week by week in four offensive and four pitching categories, and the teams are ranked by points in each category. Perception of a game is distorted by the fun-house mirror of Fantasy Ball. Winning is no longer the be-all or end-all; a three-run dinger in a 10–2 laugher for your team is worth more than a sacrifice fly to win an extra-inning game.

Critics of fantasy baseball say that it destroys team loyalty. But a fan's long-standing emotional attachment to one team has already been somewhat diluted by several factors. One is the opportunity to view other teams on television rather than just the home club, and another is the frequency with which favored players change cities in pursuit of the best deal for themselves. The Rotisserian roots for his *own* team, and if you're a fan in Cleveland, where the team may actually win a pennant once in a generation, getting to experience a fantasy pennant race can be something of a godsend.

For those who enjoy the preoccupations that Rotisserie baseball offers, fantasy ownership is felt as part of a fan's natural progression— from hero-worshipers to inside-game mavens and ultimately to armchair general managers analyzing what wins pennants—what kinds of players, in what combinations. Some will always consider the fantasy owner's endless scrutiny and tabulation of numbers to be an abomination of fandom: improper fan behavior. But the popularity of fantasy leagues arose in the '80s during a time when the baseball public at large became privy to a wealth of hitherto unknown or guarded statistical information.

A stat wizard named Bill James put out *The Baseball Abstract,* which became, much to everyone's surprise, a perennial best-seller. The same audience now eagerly awaits the publication each spring of *The Elias Baseball Analyst*. Publications like *Baseball America* cater to the interest of Rotisserie GMs in the minor leagues—which top prospects the major league organizations plan to promote, and how these phenoms might perform in the majors. And so the niche for the number-crunchers was already made, and the fantasy players filled it and made statistics their Holy Grail. But so do the real-life players when they go to arbitration with their own stat analysts and plead their cases for more money.

Fans used to be able to root for players because they liked them, not just because they "owned" their stats, and in that sense Rotisserie's popularity could be a symptom of the game's ills—the growing distance between the ballplayer and his public. It would seem that the bond that once existed between the fan and his beloved game has been forever altered when fans seek private gratifications in the daily accomplishments of their handpicked teams. Fantasy involvement may be the fans' revenge against bombastic owners, money-mad players, and the incessant media prattle and hype surrounding baseball, a way of reclaiming a part of the game for their very own.

Ultimately, fantasy ball coexists alongside the real season, as yet another meta-level, another game within the game. But when baseball becomes sufficiently compelling, the outcome easily takes precedence over whatever fantasy stats the game may generate. For the true fan, the pleasures of watching great players try to win close games in a good pennant race remain undiminished.